THE COMPLETE DICTIONARY OF MORTGAGE & LENDING TERMS EXPLAINED SIMPLY

What Smart Investors Need to Know

THE COMPLETE DICTIONARY OF MORTGAGE & LENDING TERMS EXPLAINED SIMPLY: WHAT SMART INVESTORS NEED TO KNOW

The complete dictionary of mortgage & lending terms explained simply : what smart investors need to know / by Atlantic Publishing Group, Inc.
     p. cm.
  ISBN-13: 978-1-60138-014-2 (alk. paper)
  ISBN-10: 1-60138-014-3 (alk. paper)
  1. Mortgage banks--Dictionaries. 2. Mortgage loans--Dictionaries. I. Atlantic Publishing Group.
  HG2040.C67 2010
  332.703--dc22

                        2010025160

PROJECT MANAGER: Melissa Peterson
COVER DESIGN: Jackie Miller • millerjackiej@gmail.com

Printed in the United States

Printed on Recycled Paper

We recently lost our beloved pet "Bear," who was not only our best and dearest friend but also the "Vice President of Sunshine" here at Atlantic Publishing. He did not receive a salary but worked tirelessly 24 hours a day to please his parents. Bear was a rescue dog that turned around and showered myself, my wife, Sherri, his grandparents Jean, Bob, and Nancy, and every person and animal he met (maybe not rabbits) with friendship and love. He made a lot of people smile every day.

We wanted you to know that a portion of the profits of this book will be donated to The Humane Society of the United States. *–Douglas & Sherri Brown*

The human-animal bond is as old as human history. We cherish our animal companions for their unconditional affection and acceptance. We feel a thrill when we glimpse wild creatures in their natural habitat or in our own backyard.

Unfortunately, the human-animal bond has at times been weakened. Humans have exploited some animal species to the point of extinction.

The Humane Society of the United States makes a difference in the lives of animals here at home and worldwide. The HSUS is dedicated to creating a world where our relationship with animals is guided by compassion. We seek a truly humane society in which animals are respected for their intrinsic value and where the human-animal bond is strong.

Want to help animals? We have plenty of suggestions. Adopt a pet from a local shelter, join The Humane Society and be a part of our work to help companion animals and wildlife. You will be funding our educational, legislative, investigative and outreach projects in the U.S. and across the globe.

Or perhaps you'd like to make a memorial donation in honor of a pet, friend or relative? You can through our Kindred Spirits program. And if you'd like to contribute in a more structured way, our Planned Giving Office has suggestions about estate planning, annuities, and even gifts of stock that avoid capital gains taxes.

Maybe you have land you would like to preserve as a lasting habitat for wildlife. Our Wildlife Land Trust can help you. Perhaps the land you want to share is a backyard — that's enough. Our Urban Wildlife Sanctuary Program will show you how to create a habitat for your wild neighbors.

So you see, it's easy to help animals. And The HSUS is here to help.

THE HUMANE SOCIETY
OF THE UNITED STATES.

2100 L Street NW • Washington, DC 20037 • 202-452-1100
www.hsus.org

TRADEMARK DISCLAIMER

TABLE OF CONTENTS

FOREWORD

The American educational system has always served as a model and a worldwide leader in its ability to teach fundamentals in mathematics and reading. Despite the results of our standardized tests suggesting weaknesses in certain geographic communities, our schools continue to produce professionals in all walks of life who lead the world in producing innovative solutions and new technologies.

Unfortunately, most observers would agree about the need for more financial training, as this sphere of learning is generally acquired through "on-the-job" experience. We have shown glaring weaknesses in the ability to manage a budget and make sound investment decisions, and in the government, handle our national debt.

That is one reason why *The Complete Dictionary of Mortgage & Lending Terms Explained Simply* fills a vital need for financial novices and professionals alike. Both graduates and self-made executives need tools to support them in their current careers, as the days since school, for many of us, have long past.

As the president of a national residential mortgage firm, Guaranteed Home Mortgage Company, I interact with branch managers across the nation who are looking to our corporate headquarters to provide tangible support for their operations. In the process, many of them have shown a high degree of financial sophistication, but from time to time, evidence reveals major gaps in their knowledge.

In order to effectively converse with them, we need to share a common language — a need filled by this book. When our department heads in underwriting, compliance, branch development, operations, and quality assurance distribute company-wide memos, they often use technical terms unfamiliar to some of our employees. This book helps to bridge the gap in our financial backgrounds.

Secondly, American citizens outside of the financial industry have learned all too well the dangers of poor education in this field. The amount of consumer debt we have compiled as a society shows an inability to make even the most elementary budget decisions. And, government budgetary matters also demonstrate the danger of a poor financial background.

In my field, we have seen outright fraud perpetuated through the promotion of adjustable-rate mortgages to homeowners unable to meet future obligations. Established companies such as Guaranteed suffer from these outliers who took advantage of the system, and our entire industry gets painted with a broad uncomplimentary brush as a result.

The public has suffered from a lack of financial literacy in its investment decisions in other arenas as well. Derivatives and other complicated financial products have become so esoteric only those with intimate knowledge of their workings are even able to understand the associated problems. As our societies become increasingly interconnected, it is essential to avoid misunderstandings and to be able to communicate in a clear and effective manner.

Of course, many of these issues require more targeted publications — books and trade publications, business journals, and white papers — to serve as an explanatory medium. But what happens when you are in the middle of a crucial section, and you stumble upon a word you do not understand?

Learning and reading a foreign language requires a French/English dictionary, so when you read a financial treatise, you should have the same support. When I was undergoing legal training, I could not have survived without Blackstone's Legal Dictionary. This book provides the same essential service for the financial field.

David A. Wind, J.D., M.S.
President and chief executive officer
Guaranteed Home Mortgage Company, Inc.

David Wind, an attorney, is principal and president of Guaranteed Home Mortgage Company (Guaranteed, www.ghmc.com). Previously, he served as a financial analyst of mortgage-backed securities at Citicorp Investment Bank and clerked in the real estate finance department of the New York State Attorney General's Office.

Founded in 1992, Guaranteed, a licensed mortgage investment and banking firm, comprises more than 300 mortgage professionals lending in 27 states. The company, previously named in the Inc. 500 list of the fastest growing companies in the United States, provides residential mortgage financing to a wide variety of consumers and real estate professionals.

INTRODUCTION

Nikki Roberts had accomplished a lot of things in her life. She received her bachelor's degree from a prestigious university and even graduated Summa Cum Laude. She also managed to score that primo public relations job with the firm she always admired while studying the field in college. Nikki had a wonderful husband, Desmond, who was quite successful himself. Most importantly, they made each other happy.

Even though there were some important milestones left to check off in their lives — always something new to accomplish — above all others, there was one Nikki could not get out of her head: Nikki wanted to own a home.

That dream was planted at an early age while spending so much time with her father and Uncle Joey, who was many things in life, but above all, he was someone who loved to invest in real estate. In fact, he did quite well with it. So with many of her other major goals in life checked off, Nikki decided it was time to find a house she could call her own.

Uncle Joey was getting older and, for the most part, had retired from real estate investing, but Nikki trusted his opinion in these matters above anyone else's. She went to talk to him about it because she could not find a mortgage deal that would not completely strip her of all of the luxuries. Unfortunately, due to Nikki's love for extra luxuries, her credit score was low and banks were hesitant about giving her a loan.

But never fear; Uncle Joey always had a plan. He told her the real estate market was one in which you could make a few mistakes but still end up on top because housing prices were always going up. "History never lies," he said. This gave her the confidence to take out a somewhat pricey mortgage loan — something she was a little hesitant to do. When she took those first steps into her new home, she figured it was all worth it. She knew as housing prices continued to rise, she would be able to refinance, and her monthly mortgage payment would decrease. She just had to get through the growing pains that came with taking that next big step in life.

Unfortunately, Uncle Joey's time away from the real estate market had left him a little rusty at calling his usual spot-on real estate shots. It is doubtful even he would have been able to predict the crash of the housing market in 2007. Not many people did. As the economy started to teeter and eventually fall flat on its face, Nikki and Desmond had to take pay cuts to keep their jobs. In fact, they were lucky to *have* jobs. Many of their friends did not. Where they were not lucky, though, was in their standing with the mortgage.

Nikki never really understood all that nonsense Stu, her mortgage broker, was spewing at her when she signed her name on the dotted line. So, when Stu told her there was no way she would ever refinance her loan, she was devastated.

Nikki and Desmond had to surrender the house just to survive. They rented a small apartment and did not get a good night sleep for quite a while after seeing the "For Sale" sign in their front yard. Nikki vowed never again to go into a deal without knowing more than her adversary sitting across the table. If things work out for her the way they did once upon a time, she might get that chance again.

Many people who were crushed in the 2007 housing market crash did not fully understand what they were getting themselves into when they signed their name to the mortgage documents. But you do not have to be one of those people. With *The Complete Dictionary of Mortgage & Lending Terms Explained Simply* in hand, you can easily translate every phrase that comes flying off your real estate agent and broker's tongue.

With easy-to-understand definitions, this dictionary covers everything from accrued interest to wraparound mortgages. It covers types of mortgages, parts of loan agreements, types of insurance, and even home-inspection terms. This resource uses simple language to describe the many concepts it details, which ensures even those without any financial or real estate experience will understand the definitions. With more than 1,800 terms, this dictionary allows you to understand almost every term you come across during your encounter with the lending process, whether you are researching the difference between trusts and liens or examining a prospective home's features. In addition to outlining terms associated with lending, it also includes information about important legislative acts and federal agencies that affect financing. The handy A-to-Z organization allows you to quickly find any information you need, even during nerve-wracking negotiations.

Whether you are looking to buy a home, trying to refinance, taking a finance class, or simply curious about the mortgage and lending industry, this dictionary is an indispensable guide to the many terms, tools, and agreements you will encounter at every step of the complex lending process.

3/2 down payment: A program that allows a borrower who secures money through a grant or gift equal to 2 percent of the down payment to only pay a 3-percent down payment of his or her own

3.95% ARM: A monthly ARM that has a 3.95 percent initial rate

12-Month Treasury Average (12 MTA): An index used to measure the interest rate on some ARMs. It is made up of the 12-month averages of U.S. Treasuries' monthly yields, then adjusted to a one-year constant maturity value.

100% loan: A type of loan in which the amount is equal to the property value and which requires no down payment

125% loan: A type of loan given for 125 percent of the value of the property

40-year mortgage: A mortgage spanning the length of 40 years

A

Abandonment: When an owner or renter gives up their property and leaves without passing ownership or tenancy rights to anyone else. The abandoner still owes any debts related to the property unless the owed party cancels them. Abandoned properties are reclaimed by lenders or other entities with a prior interest.

Abatement: A lowering of rent fees or another reduction benefiting the tenant, such as free rent, early move-in, or removal of a harmful substance like asbestos.

Abnormal sale: When a house or property sells for more or less than its current market value — for instance, 25 percent less than comparable homes nearby. Appraisers can ignore abnormal sales when comparing similar properties for value.

Absentee owner: Someone who owns a property without managing it or living on-site. He or she might hire another person to oversee it.

Absolute liability: Liability associated with dangerous actions. The actions leading to the liability do not have to be proven negligent, just different than public policy.

Absorption rate: How quickly homes sell or rental spaces gain occupants. Calculate this percentage by dividing the total number of homes or square feet of rental space in an area by the number purchased or filled during a given time period.

Abstract of title: The summarized history of a piece of real estate. It describes each time the property changed hands and notes all encumbrances that have lessened its value or use. This document is certified as complete and truthful by the abstractor.

Abut: To be adjacent. A property can abut — border — landmarks such as roads and easements. When one property meets or joins another, the line between is an abutment.

A-credit: A consumer with a credit rating that far surpasses average, which therefore warrants the lowest prices lenders can offer. Consumers with a Fair Isaac Corporation (FICO®) score greater than 720 qualify as A-credit by most lenders' standards.

Acceleration clause: Part of a rental contract that says a lender can insist a borrower pay the balance of the loan right away under certain circumstances. A lender might invoke this clause if the renter defaults on the loan or seriously delays payments.

Acceptance: Completion of a sales contract when someone offers to buy a property under specific terms and the owner accepts.

Accessory building: Serves a different function from the main building on a lot. Accessory buildings include garages, but they do not include separate structures for commercial use.

Accident: An unplanned occurrence outside the control of the insured that happens suddenly and due to pure chance.

Accord and satisfaction: An agreement settling a debt. A creditor considers the debt repaid after accepting a different or smaller compensation than the debtor originally promised. Such an accord can end a dispute.

Accountant: The person responsible for helping the agent file his or her taxes and keep up with tax obligations.

Accredited advisor in insurance: An agent or other individual who has completed the three exams administered by the Insurance Institute of America.

Accredited investor: A private investor deemed wealthy enough to be able to afford losses on risky private offerings.

Accrued depreciation (accumulated depreciation): The current sum of all depreciation expenses.

Accrued interest: Interest accumulated over a certain amount of time but is neither due nor paid yet; accrued interest adds to the amount already owed.

Accrued items, active: Expenses paid early for things in the next business year. For example, people can prepay rent for buildings they will occupy the following year.

Accrued items, passive: Expenses incurred that cannot be paid yet, such as taxes on real estate and interest on loans.

Acknowledgment: When someone formally declares they have signed a document before a notary public or another appropriately authorized person.

Acquisition appraisal: When a government agency determines how much to pay a property owner after acquiring their property via negotiation or condemnation.

Acquisition cost: The total price someone pays for a property, with all fees added in.

Acre: Equal to 43,560 square feet (4,840 square yards), an acre is the standard area unit for measuring property.

Acreage zoning (large-lot or "snob" zoning): Zoning calling for large lots, meant to make commercial or residential areas less dense.

Act of God: When a natural disaster humans cannot control, such as an earthquake, severe storm, or flood, strikes a property; contracts can include provisions relieving all those involved from obligation.

Actual cash value: The cash value of an improvement for insurance purposes. It equals the cost of replacing something minus the wear and tear.

Actual damages (and special damages): Actual damages are legally determined costs for repairing something wrongfully harmed or destroyed. Special damages include indirect effects of the property destruction, such as lessened income to a business in a damaged building.

Ad valorem tax: Latin for "according to value." A tax pertaining to the financial worth of the property being taxed. These collected taxes usually benefit the city, county, or school district.

ADC loan: Acquisition, development, and construction loan. Developers use ADC loans to buy property, install utilities and roads, and erect buildings.

Add-backs: Extraordinary one-time expenses, such as the cost of moving. Add-backs are subject to acute scrutiny by the buyer because travel and entertainment are usually regular costs of doing business.

Addendum: An amendment or revision to a contract both parties consent to and sign.

Addition: Making a building larger through further construction. Additions do not include improvements, such as finishing unfinished rooms.

Additional insured: A second beneficiary added to the same policy; for example, the children of the insured.

Additional living expense: Typically found in a homeowner's policy. This coverage provides reimbursement of expenses incurred while the insured is forced to live outside his or her home temporarily; for example, the cost of temporary lodging or eating in restaurants.

Adhesion insurance contract: A contract offered on a "take it or leave it" basis.

Adjudication: A decision made in court.

Adjustable-rate mortgage (ARM): Unlike a fixed-rate loan, this home loan has a changing interest rate, which fluctuates to stay current with rates of mortgage loans. It can also change with indexes of the government or financial market.

Adjusted funds from operations (AFFO): A measurement of a real estate company's available funds generated by operations. The first part of the calculation subtracts the REIT's Funds From Operations (FFO) from normalized recurring expenditures capitalized by the REIT and then amortized, but which are essential to uphold a REIT's revenue stream and properties. That includes items such as new carpeting in apartment units and leasing expenses. The second facet for calculating AFFO is to subtract what is known as the "straight-lining" of rents from the FFO. A REIT's AFFO is also known as Cash Available for Distribution (CAD).

Adjusted premium: A premium composed of a net level premium and an amount defined as the first year's acquisition expenses divided by the current value of a life annuity due.

Adjustment date: A specific day when the interest rate for an adjustable-rate mortgage changes.

Adjustment interval: The period between the alterations in an adjustable-rate mortgage (ARM)'s monthly payment or interest rate. The adjustment interval is typically shown as the ratio of X/Y, where "X" is the amount of time until the initial modification on the rate, and "Y" is the period of adjustment after the first modification is made. For instance, a 7/1 ARM occurs when the initial rate is the same for seven years but is adjusted every year after that. On a fully amortizing ARM, the adjustment intervals for rate and payment are the same; this may not be the case with a negative amortization ARM.

Adjustment period: For an adjustable-rate mortgage, this is the time period between changes in interest rate.

Adjustment provision: A clause that allows the policy to be changed by increasing or decreasing the premium or face amount. Also can be changed by extending or decreasing the duration of protection or premiums.

Administrator: A court-appointed person who settles the estate of a person who dies with no will.

Admitted company: A company licensed to provide insurance in a particular state.

Advance fee: Money clients pay before receiving services. Real estate agents can charge homeowners an advance fee to foot advertising bills while selling the property.

Adverse financial change condition: This provision lets a lender cancel a loan agreement if the borrower loses his or her job or has other serious financial troubles.

Adverse financial selection: When a policyholder surrenders the policy for cash due to financial need or because the money can be better invested elsewhere.

Adverse possession: Blatantly and aggressively occupying another person's land and claiming entitlement without permission from the owner. Adverse possession does not include leasing property with an owner's consent or occupying property of unknown ownership.

Adverse selection: When an individual who is a higher-than-average risk tries to buy insurance at the standard rate.

Adviser: An investment banker or a broker representing a property owner during a real estate transaction. The adviser collects a fee when transaction or financing ends.

Aesthetic value: Worth of a property determined by its beauty.

Affidavit of title: A statement written under oath by a real estate grantor or seller and recognized by a notary public. The person gives his or her identity, confirms the title has not changed for the worse since it was last examined, and officially declares he or she possesses the property (if appropriate).

Affirmation: A way to declare a statement true without swearing an oath if someone has religious or other objections to giving oaths.

Affordability: When a house's price is within the financial means of a consumer. Affordability is generally represented by the absolute highest price the consumer can pay for a house while being authorized for the mortgage necessary to pay that price.

Affordability index: A measure designed by the National Association of Realtors® to describe how affordable houses are for residents buying in a given area.

Affordable housing: Public or private programs helping low-income people afford houses. These efforts can provide low-interest home loans, smaller down payments, and less demanding credit terms.

After-repair value (ARV): Used to determine a property's true value after repairs have been taken care of on the property in question.

Agency: A relationship in which principal brokers — leaders of brokerage firms — allow agents to represent them in specific transactions.

Agency by ratification: When the insurance company accepts the actions of an agent, this ratifies the act and makes the company liable for consequences that may occur.

Agency disclosure: An agreement most states require. Real estate agents who serve sellers and buyers must disclose whom they are representing.

Agent: Someone acting on another's behalf under the law of agency. Property owners authorize licensed real estate brokers to be their agents.

Aggregate annual deductible: A deductible that applies for the entire year.

Aggregate limit: The maximum amount of coverage available to the insured during a certain period, regardless of the number of accidents during that period.

Agreed amount clause: A clause that states the amount of insurance will automatically meet the coinsurance clause.

Agreement of sale: A legal document giving the terms and price of a property sale that both parties sign.

Alienation clause: Found in a mortgage or deed of trust, this clause prevents the borrower from selling the property — and transferring the associated debt — to another person without the lender's permission. If the borrower sells, the lender can immediately demand full repayment of the debt.

Alienation: Property going to a new owner by sale, gift, adverse possession, or eminent domain.

Alien insurer: An insurer formed under the laws of a different country than the one it operates in.

Alt-A: A category of mortgage risk classified between sub-prime and prime but falls closer to prime; also known as "A minus."

Alternative documentation: This is sometimes referred to as limited doc, which means less documentation is needed to secure a loan. The good thing about these loans is the time for approval is generally less. The borrower will need to have excellent or good credit and meet income requirements for the past two years to qualify for these loans.

Alliance of American Insurers: A group of insurers who work together in areas of common interest, such as government affairs, education of employees, and loss prevention.

Allocation of purchase price: The purchase price in an asset sale must be budgeted among certain assets; the balance is goodwill.

Alluvion: Soil deposit that builds up on a property and is considered the owner's possession.

Amenities: Advantages to owning a property not related to money, or features that make it more desirable.

American agency system: Also known as the independent agency system, a system in which insurance is sold through independent agents.

American Insurance Association: A group of property and liability insurance companies that promotes the standing of its members.

Americans with Disabilities Act (ADA): Designed to ensure disabled people have equal access to public accommodations and transportation, jobs, telecommunications, and government services. Covers design of public buildings.

Amortization: Paying off a debt and its interest in gradual installments.

Amortization schedule: A charted timetable for paying off a loan that shows how much of each payment goes toward interest and toward the debt itself. It also shows the continual decline of the loan until the balance reaches zero.

Amortization term: Amount of time needed to pay off, or amortize, a loan.

Amortized note: A promissory note paid off entirely in installments.

Amount financed: In terms of the Truth in Lending Act, the amount financed is the entire loan amount minus all lender fees, which are paid at closing (known as "prepaid finance charges"). For example, if someone borrows a loan of $90,000 and he or she pays the lender $3,000 in fees, the amount financed ends up being $87,000.

Anchor tenant: The person or business that draws the most visitors to a commercial property, such as a supermarket among other stores.

Angels: An individual high-risk investor who likes to make investments in promising acquisitions. Angels often have valuable business experience and can be helpful as members of a board of directors.

Annexation: A city expanding its borders to encompass a certain area. Most states require public approval first, demonstrated by holding votes in the city and the area it will annex. Annexation also denotes personal property becoming part of real property.

Annual aggregate limit: The annual limit up to which a policy will cover regardless of how many claims are made.

Annual debt service: The yearly payments a person must make on a loan, which comprises the principle and interest added over 12 months.

Annual percentage rate (APR): The actual interest rate of a loan for a year, which might be higher than the rate advertised. It must be disclosed in accordance with the Truth in Lending Act.

Annual statement: A report of the insurer's finances submitted to the state insurance department.

Apartment association: A group of apartment owners who meet at a scheduled time to determine the needs of the property in question and decide on general maintenance issues.

Apartments and multifamily housing: Apartment buildings are residential structures comprising five or more units in a single building or a series of buildings. Multifamily housing is used to describe four or fewer residential units.

Appleton rule: A rule requiring every insurer in New York to comply with the New York Insurance Code, even in other states.

Application: The form required to borrow money for a home loan.

Application fee: Money charged to the borrower at the time of the application. This is generally a flat fee meant to cover the lender's cost for processing the application. It is often included in the closing costs.

Appointed actuary: An actuary appointed by an insurance company charged with documenting the liability reserve of an insurer.

Appointments: Items in a building that may enhance or lessen how valuable or functional the property is. Examples include furniture, equipment, and fixtures.

Apportionment: Dividing yearly costs associated with a property between the seller and the buyer. Each party pays expenses such as insurance or taxes for the portion of the year they owned the property.

Apportionment clause: A clause that requires claims on a property to be divided among all insurance policies covering that property.

Appraisal: Determines a property's estimated market value.

Appraisal clause: Clause that gives either party (the insured or the insurer) the right to an appraisal to determine the value of a loss.

Appraisal fee: What an appraiser charges for doing the appraisal on a property. This fee can vary but is often between $300 and $400.

Appraisal report: The report an appraiser writes describing a property's value and summarizing how it was determined.

Appraised value: The monetary value of a property given in an appraisal report.

Appraiser: A person who is licensed to prepare appraisals for real estate transactions. The Federal Housing Administration (FHA) uses an FHA-approved list.

Appreciation: The process of a home or property gaining value, which can stem from several factors including additions to the building, changes in financial markets, and inflation.

Appropriation: Reserving land for public access, which might be required before development projects can progress.

Approval: A borrower's loan application acceptance, which means the borrower meets qualification and underwriting requirements set forth by the lender. If approval is given via an automated underwriting system, the borrower may have to verify certain information before their application can be approved.

Appurtenance: A privilege, right, or benefit tied to a piece of land without being physically part of the property. One example is the right to access someone else's land.

Appurtenant easement: The right, belonging to a parcel's owner, to use a neighbor's property.

Appurtenant structure: A secondary structure on the insured premises.

Arbitration: When two parties use an impartial third entity to resolve a dispute instead of going to court. Real estate contracts can require arbitration, which prevents lawsuits.

Arbitration clause: A clause stating that in case of a disagreement regarding the amount of a claim, each party (the insured and the insurer) will appoint an appraiser, who will then select an umpire. An amount will then be determined by at least two of the three, and this settlement will be binding.

Architecture: All facets of building construction, from materials, tools, and methods to elements of design and style.

Area: A space defined by two dimensions: length and width. Multiplying length by width yields the area of a lot or floor.

ARM (adjustable-rate mortgage) index: An openly published number that guides how adjustable-rate mortgages change.

Arm's length transaction: A deal in which each party protects its own interests above all.

Arrears: A payment made "in arrears" is given at the end of a month or other term. Late or defaulted payments can also be described as in arrears.

Artesian well: A vertical tunnel to access water naturally springing from underground.

As-built drawings: Illustrations showing exactly how a building was constructed, including alterations to the original plans and the position of utilities and equipment.

Asbestos: This mineral, formerly common in insulation and other building materials, is now prohibited because it causes lung disease.

Asbestos-containing materials (ACM): Prohibited because of health hazards since the early 1980s, materials containing asbestos still are found in certain old buildings.

"As is" condition: A term in real estate contracts meaning the buyer or renter accepts the property and its flaws just as they are and gives up the right to insist on repairs or renovations.

Asking (advertised) price: The amount a property owner hopes a buyer will pay, which may change with negotiation.

Assessable insurance: A policy under which a first premium is assessed and a second premium may be assessed later if the insurance company's losses exceed their premium income.

Assessed value: The value a tax assessor determines a home to have, which is used for computing a tax base.

Assessment company: An insurer who may charge insured parties extra if the premiums already paid are not enough to cover their operating costs.

Assessment insurance: A policy wherein extra costs can be assessed to the policyholder should the insurer's loss experience be worse than expected.

Assessment valuation: The value intended for property taxes. Those taxes depend on the amount assessed, usually the tax amount per $100 of value. The assessment ratio is the relationship between estimated value and market value.

Assessor: A public official responsible for valuing properties for tax purposes.

Asset: A valuable possession or property.

Asset-based lenders: Commercial lenders who do not mind taking on more risk than commercial banks in terms of lending against inventory and accounts receivable and being secondary to commercial banking institutions.

Asset depreciation risk: The risk that the assets of a company may lose market value over time.

Asset management: All aspects of handling real estate assets from when someone first invests in them until they sell them.

Asset sale: Buying specific assets and/or liabilities, leaving the remainder to the seller and the corporate entity.

Asset valuation: The net profit or loss of a premium after deducting the insurance and expenses.

Asset valuation reserve: A reserve composed of all invested assets of all classes. This reserve is made mandatory by the National Association of Insurance Commissioners (NAIC).

Assignment: Handing over the responsibilities and rights associated with a property to another, as a landlord does to a paying tenant. If that recipient fails to pay, the original party absorbs the debt.

Assignment clause: A clause that allows the holder of a policy to sell or give the policy to another person or company.

Assignment of lease: Passing off the rights to use a leased property from one renter to another. For instance, a person who occupies an apartment for part of the year may recruit someone else to live there when he or she is gone.

Assignment of rents: A contract saying a tenant's rent payments will go to the owner's mortgage lender if the owner defaults.

Assignor: Someone who passes a property's interests and rights to a new recipient.

Associate broker (broker-associates, affiliate brokers, or broker-salespersons): A real estate broker supervised by another broker. This manager holds the associate broker's license.

Association of unit owners: An organization of condominium owners that oversees the property where the owners live.

Association or syndicate pool: A group of insurers who write a large risk together and have an agreement to split the premiums and expenses.

Assumable mortgage: This mortgage loan can be shifted from borrower to borrower.

Assumption: Buying another's mortgage.

Assumption clause: Part of the contract drawn when a mortgage changes hands. This makes the party buying the mortgage loan responsible for it.

Assumption fee: Money one must pay when buying another's mortgage to cover the costs of processing the paperwork.

Attachment: A person's possessions that legal authorities seize when the person fails to pay a debt. For example, landlords attach items their tenants own to unpaid rent.

Attest: To observe an event and sign a document certifying you witnessed it.

Attestation clause: Clause that requires the officers of an insurance company to sign a contract in order for it to be completed.

Attic: Space between the top story's ceiling and the roof that people can access. Conversely, a structural cavity is a similar space that people cannot enter.

Attorney-in-fact: Someone who can legally act on another's behalf, which can mean selling the other party's property.

Attorney's opinion of title: A summarized history of a piece of real estate that an attorney has scrutinized and declared valid in his or her opinion.

Attornment: A legal agreement in which tenants formally accept a new landlord by signing a letter of attornment.

Auction: Selling personal property or land to the highest bidder. States can do this with foreclosed property. Bidders can make public or private offers in writing or speech.

Auctioneer: Licensed person who carries out auctions of real estate or other property.

Audit: Examination of financial records and accounting books in order to verify their accuracy.

Authorized user: A person other than the original holder of the credit card who is allowed to use the same credit card. The main cardholder is accountable for everything the authorized user charges; therefore, the authorized user does not have to pay any charges he or she made. However, sometimes it is insisted that the authorized user pay the cardholder's unpaid bills.

Authorization to sell: Contract licensing a real estate agent to sell one's property. The agent can advertise the property and collect a fee for selling it but cannot make the final agreement to sell.

Automated underwriting system: A method of doing electronic underwriting via a computerized machine. Many big companies and mortgage insurers have begun using these systems, including Fannie Mae and Freddie Mac. These computer systems allow lenders to approve loans faster and reduce the costs of lending.

Automatic coverage: Coverage automatically provided under an existing policy to cover newly purchased property or property that appreciates in value.

Automatic extension: A clause found in a listing agreement; an accord a property owner makes with a real estate broker that says the owner will pay the broker to lease or sell property for a given price. An automatic extension makes the listing agreement persist after it expires for a specified time. Certain states forbid or discourage using automatic extensions.

Automatic reinstatement clause: A clause stating the original policy limit will be reinstated after partial losses covered by the policy have been paid.

Average occupancy: The percentage of time a property was occupied in the last year. To calculate, divide the number of months it was occupied by 12.

B

Back-end fee or commission: The income of a mortgage broker that the lender pays.

Backup offer: A second buyer offers to purchase or lease property if the current buyer cannot follow through. When the first buyer backs out, the backup offer takes effect.

Bad credit loans: Loans made to borrowers with poor credit. The interest rate is generally higher than for borrowers with good credit.

"Bad-faith estimate": Luring in people shopping for mortgages with a low-ball estimate on settlement costs of the Good Faith Estimate. The low estimate makes the figure seem more appealing to potential consumers.

Bailee's customer insurance: Insurance that covers the bailee, the person temporarily in possession of another property, in case of damage to the property while under his or her care.

The bailee is covered against many potential hazards, including fire damage, theft, robbery, and sprinkler leaks.

Bailout: Support provided by the government to a business or other organization in financial trouble; designed to protect creditors and the business' employees.

Balance: Debt unpaid. Appraisers also use balance to describe a situation when a property's improvements are proportional to the land and to each other, making the property's value peak.

Balance sheet: A list of someone's net worth, assets, and liabilities.

Balloon loan: A mortgage with monthly payments followed by a large final payment, which covers the remaining debt. For example, after five years' worth of making monthly payments, your "balloon" (the balance) would be due.

Balloon payment: The large, final payment in a balloon mortgage loan, which covers the debt not paid in earlier installments.

Bankruptcy: A court proceeding during which an individual or business is offered relief from debts the person or business cannot pay. Chapter 7 bankruptcy is known as liquidation, and the assets of the debtor are sold to pay creditors. Chapter 11 bankruptcy is used in businesses for reorganization, and the owner continues to operate the business while repaying creditors on a schedule approved by the court. Chapter 13 is a repayment plan in which an individual agrees to make partial payments over a period of three to five years. This requires the individual to file a budget with the court.

Bargain and sale deed: Gives the grantor the right to convey title without making warranties against encumbrances or liens, but the grantor can attach warranties if desired. *See definitions of "lien" and "encumbrance" for further information.*

Base loan amount: Sum of money forming the basic payments on a loan.

Base premium: An insurance company's premium upon which the reinsurance premium is based.

Base principal balance: Version of the original loan sum adjusted based on principal payments and later funding. It excludes other unsettled debts and accumulated interest.

Basic form rates: As put forth under the commercial lines program, Group I and Group II rates combine to form the basic form rates.

Basic limit: The minimum amount for which a liability policy can be written.

Basic limits of liability: The minimum amount for which a liability policy can be written, as dictated by the published rates or the law.

Basic mortality table: A table listing the actual ages of death of a population with no adjustments made for probability.

Basic premium: A fraction of the standard premium. This portion is used for administrative costs and agent commissions.

Basis point: A term financial markets use to mean 1/100 of a percent.

Basket: A dollar amount set forth by the seller in the indemnification provision for any losses suffered by the buyer.

Below grade: A building or part existing below the ground surface.

Benchmark: A permanent mark carefully measured to show height, which surveyors use to begin their surveys or measure the elevation of a site.

Beneficiary: Someone who gets or is entitled to benefits, such as a person receiving income from a trust fund. A beneficiary can also be the lender of a deed of trust loan.

Beneficiary clause: Clause that allows the insured to designate anyone as a beneficiary and to change this designation at any time.

Beneficiary of trust: A person for whom a trust has been created and who will eventually receive the benefits of said trust.

Benefit: An amount paid to a beneficiary of an insurance policy or the participant of a retirement plan.

Bequeath: To leave possessions to certain recipients in one's will. For passing on real estate in a will, use the term "devise."

Betterment: Any actions improving a piece of real estate.

Bill of sale: A document that legally transfers personal property — not a real estate title — to a new owner.

Bimonthly mortgage: A type of mortgage where the borrower pays twice in the same month. Half the payment is paid on the first day of the month and half is paid on the 15th.

Binder: An agreement signifying that a buyer wants to join a real estate contract. The buyer might also make a payment to show earnest desire and ability to purchase the property.

Binding receipt: Proof of a temporary contract, which forces a property insurance company to provide coverage provided a premium is paid with the application.

Binomial distribution: A function used to predict the probability of future events.

Bird dog: A person who tries to locate properties for an individual investor in exchange for a fee.

Biweekly mortgage: A plan to make payments on a mortgage every two weeks. When debtors pay half the monthly fee every two weeks, they end up supplying 13 months' payment over a year, which settles the debt faster.

Blanket insurance: In property insurance, a contract that covers either several types of property in a single location, or several types of property at many locations.

Blanket limit: Maximum amount of coverage a company will write in a particular area.

Blanket loan: This mortgage covers multiple pieces of real estate but partially frees each parcel from the mortgage lien when certain fractions of the debt are repaid.

Blanket rate: The amount of premiums charged for blanket insurance covering properties at more than one location.

Blemished borrowers: These borrowers possess one or more of the following risky characteristics: they can make little or no down payment, their property consists of something different than a home for a single family, they are unable to report the entirety of their assets or income, their credit scores are lower than they should be, they have low income compared to their total expected expenses, and their adjustable mortgage rate is such that could result in considerably higher payments in the future.

Blended insurance program: A long-term program that combines many types of insurance, including finite risk, reinsurance, and traditional insurance.

Blighted areas: Part of a city or other area where the buildings are run down or needing repair.

Blind pool: A commingled real estate fund that will bring in investment capital without going through an analysis of property assets.

Block limits: Maximum amount of insurance an insurance company will write on a specific city block.

Block of policies: The total number of policies written by one insurance company using the same policy forms and rates.

Blue-sky statutes: State laws that govern the sale of securities.

Blueprint: Working set of thorough guidelines for a construction project.

Board of Realtors®: Licensed real estate professionals belonging to the state and National Association of Realtors®.

Bona fide: Considered free from fraud, such as a contract verified by a notary public.

Bond: A debt instrument issued by the U.S. government, an organization, or other institution to raise money, typically for a specific project.

Book of business: A book totaling all insurance written by a company or agent.

Book value: A property's worth as determined by its purchase price and upgrades or additions minus any depreciation. Corporations use it to indicate their properties' values.

Boot: Consideration for a tax-free transfer of property, usually money or other property.

Borderline risk: An applicant of doubtful quality, according to underwriting standards.

Borrower (mortgager): The party or parties who apply for a mortgage to finance the purchase or refinance real estate property. They are responsible for repaying the loan (mortgage) to the lender.

Boston plan: A plan under which insurers have agreed not to reject providing coverage to residences in slum areas. Coverage is extended until there has been an inspection and the owner has had a chance to correct imperfections.

Bottom fishing: When a buyer will only pay a low price for a business.

Bottomry: An insurance contract that accepts a ship or its cargo as collateral for a loan funding a maritime voyage. In the event the ship is lost, the loan is cancelled, and the borrower is not obligated to repay the lender.

Boundary: The border around a property.

Branch office: An outlying arm of a real estate business separate from the main office, where licensed brokers work on behalf of the headquarters.

Breach of contract: Breaking terms of a contract in a legally inexcusable way.

Break-even ratio: The point in time when income equals expenses.

Bridge insurance: Insurance that covers a structural bridge in the event of damage or destruction.

Bridge insurance for bridges under construction: Insurance that covers a bridge against fire damage, lightning strike, earthquake, collision, flood, and other acts of God while the bridge is in the process of construction.

Bridge loan (gap loan, swing loan, or interim financing): A short-term loan taken out between mortgages or used by those still looking for a more enduring loan. It can be useful for buildings under construction.

Broad evidence rule: Rule applied to calculating the actual cash value of lost property. Under this rule, any evidence about the value of the item is considered admissible. The item's value can also be determined by any means that accurately depict its true value.

Broad form: Insurance that covers many hazards, including theft, loss, property damage, and vandalism.

Broad form cause of loss: A type of homeowner's insurance wherein most reasons for a loss are covered.

Broker: Someone paid to liaise between sellers and buyers.

Broker agent: A person who acts as a broker for some insurers and an agent for others.

Brokerage: A group or corporation of brokers. Also means the broker industry.

Brokerage business: Business brought in by a broker to an insurance company.

Brokerage department: The department within an insurer that places insurance with brokers.

Brokerage fee: The fee earned by a broker for selling a company's insurance.

Brokerage general agent: An independent agent who sells the insurance company's products to brokers so the brokers can then sell them to the public. This person is charged with appointing brokers on behalf of the company.

Brokerage supervisor: An insurance company employee authorized to designate insurance company brokers.

Brownfield: A property on which people once used hazardous substances, such as a vacant gas station or closed factory.

Brownstone: A row house adjoining other buildings that stands three to five stories tall.

Budget mortgage: The debtor pays extra money for insurance, real estate taxes, or other fees beyond the basic payments — principal and interest. Not paying these added fees could bring foreclosure. The lender sets this money aside in an escrow account until the taxes or other fees need to be paid. Budget mortgages are used for conventional residential mortgages as well as loans guaranteed by the Department of Veterans Affairs or the Federal Housing Administration.

Buffer zone: A piece of land separating two properties with different purposes. Buffer zones are parks or are used in similar ways.

Build to suit: A landowner pays to construct a building suited to a tenant's needs, then the tenant leases it. Used for tenants who want to do business in specific type of building without owning it.

Build-out: Upgrades made to real estate following a tenant's orders.

Buildable acres: Proportion of land buildings can occupy considering how much space will go to roads, open areas, setbacks, or spots not suitable for construction.

Builder's risk coverage forms: Insurance coverage for buildings currently under construction.

Builder-financed construction: Construction for which the builder provides the funds for completion.

Building code: Local laws describing how people can use a given property, including what types of construction, building materials, and improvements are legal. Building inspectors make sure people comply.

Building efficiency ratio: The relationship between the net leasable area as compared to the gross leasable area.

Building line (setback): A border that is a set distance from a lot's sides and that shows where people may not construct buildings.

Building permit: Document giving permission for people to build, alter, or demolish improvements to buildings. It abides by zoning laws and building codes.

Building restrictions: Specify what sizes, locations, and appearances a building can legally have, as part of a building code.

Building standards: Themes the developer or owner of a building uses in its construction, such as certain types of windows or doors.

Bulk sale: A buyer purchases an entire group of real estate assets in different locations.

Bureau insurer: An insurance company that has joined a rating bureau, usually due to a lack of insurance company experience in a certain type of risk.

Burning ratio: The amount of losses suffered as compared to the amount of insurance in effect.

Business and personal property coverage form: Coverage for buildings and property contained within them.

Business income coverage form: Coverage against losses that occur due to property damage; for example, loss of business.

Business insurance: Insurance written for businesses. Can refer to health insurance or life insurance written for the principals of a company.

Business owner's policy: A policy that provides liability and property coverage for small businesses.

Business property and liability insurance package: Insurance for business-owned property against damage or loss by fire or vandalism. Also covers bodily injury or damage to the property caused by representatives of the business.

Business risk: A risk to the company's earning capability.

Buy-back agreement: A contract term saying the seller will purchase a property back if certain events happen.

Buy-back deductible: A deductible that can be eliminated by the payment of an extra premium.

Buy-down: Lowering a buyer's interest rate on his or her mortgage during the loan's beginning years. To do this, the seller or builder gives the buyer "discount points," which he or she pays the lender, and the lender lowers the monthly payments.

Buy-down mortgage: A home loan in which the seller or builder pays a lender to lower mortgage payments for the party who bought the property.

Buy-up: The act of paying a higher interest rate over a specified term while receiving a rebate from the lender to decrease immediate costs.

Buyer's agent: A real estate agent who acts in the interest of someone looking to purchase property and owes that party common-law or statutory agency duties.

Buyer's broker: This broker represents someone looking to buy residential real estate and owes that party common-law or statutory agency duties, as a buyer's agent does.

Buyer's expenses: The expenses paid by the borrower for the purchase of a property. These include fees for document stamps, recording the deed, attorney's fees, appraisals, inspection, surveys, title insurance, and escrow fees.

Buyer's remorse: Anxious feeling someone has after purchasing a home.

Buyers' market: A situation where buyers can be choosy about real estate and shrewd about pricing because there are more properties than buyers. That happens when economies slow, when too many buildings are constructed, or when population numbers fall.

Bylaws: Regulations a condominium association sets and uses as a guideline to conduct association business.

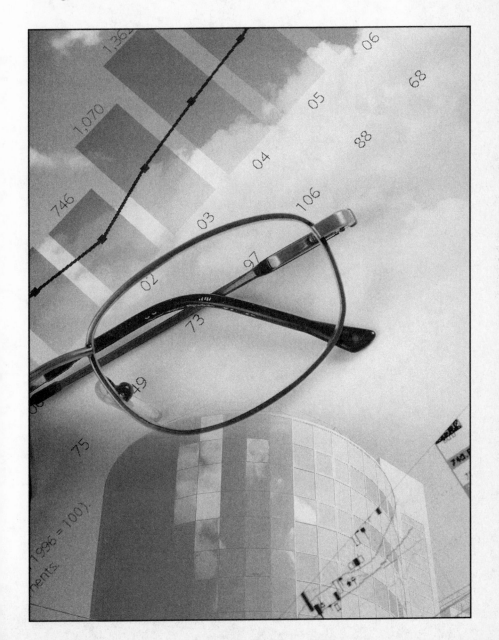

C

C-Corporation: The Internal Revenue Service code for a corporation that forms under Subchapter C provisions. This entity, commonly referred to as a C-Corp, can be either privately or publicly held and is obligated to pay taxes on its net taxable income. Its shareholders also must pay income tax on any dividends.

Call: To announce that the debt in its entirety is due at once.

Cancel: The ending of a policy, as dictated by the terms of the contract.

Cancellation clause: A contract term saying that, if certain things happen, the contract becomes void. For instance, if someone sells property he has been renting out, this clause cancels the lease.

Cap: Prevents an adjustable-rate mortgage's interest rate from growing past a certain amount. It guards the borrower against skyrocketing monthly payments.

Cap rate: The percentage at which a future flow of income changes to a present value figure.

Cap-X: The acronym for capital expenditures that are necessary within the next year.

Capacity: The largest quantity of insurance or reinsurance available for purchase, either from one company or from the entire market.

Capacity of parties: Legal competency of each party to enter in a contract.

Capital appreciation: Growth in a property's value, once partial sales and capital improvements are accounted for. It differs from a capital gain, which one receives by selling the property.

Capital gain: Extra money gained when someone sells a property for more than they paid to buy it.

Capital improvements: Bouts of spending that improve or preserve a property, such as adding useful buildings.

Capital: To a real estate agent, capital means cash or the capacity to exchange assets for money.

Capitalization rates: A method of determining a commercial real estate property's risk level. A cap rate is figured out by dividing a property's post-expenses net operating income by its purchase price. The higher the cap rate, the higher the return potential, as well as the risk. The lower the cap rate, the lower the perceived risk. So, a property with an annual net operating income of, say, $100,000 and an asking price of $1 million would have a 10 percent cap rate.

Captive agent: An agent who represents one insurance company exclusively.

Captive insurance company: A company formed exclusively to insure a parent company.

Cargo insurance: Insurance that covers cargo as it is transported to another location.

Carrier: Another term for insurer. Insurer is used more often because carrier can also mean a transportation carrier.

Carryback financing: A seller helps a buyer finance the purchase of property — for instance, by loaning the buyer money to pay the mortgage lender.

Cash (or funds) available for distribution (CAD or FAD): A REIT's ability to make cash and to administer dividends to its shareholders. This measurement is determined by subtracting nonrecurring expenditures from a REIT's FFO, on top of subtracting normalized recurring real estate-related expenditures and other noncash items.

Cash cow: A business for which the earnings have remained almost the same for the past five years and has a steady cash flow but has shown little growth.

Cash flow: How much income an investment pays, minus expenses. Positive cash flow is when there is enough income to cover the expenses. Cash flow is negative if expenses are larger than the income.

Cash flow underwriting: A method of maximizing interest earned on premiums through rating and premium collection.

Cash out of vested benefits: Money taken out of benefits by an employee.

Cash-out refinance: The practice by a borrower of refinancing his or her mortgage at an amount significantly higher than the current loan balance with the intent to use part of the money for personal use.

Cash yield on cost (CYC): A company's net operating income or its operating property revenues minus operating expenses. When used properly, it is a good measurement of a company's return on assets or the money it has invested in a given property.

Cash-out refinance: Refinancing a mortgage for more money than it originally covered to use the extra money for personal purposes. The amount of cash a borrower can take depends on several factors, including the value of the home and the amount of the mortgage, income, and credit. The borrower receives this money in a check after closing.

Cashier's check: Preferable for real estate deals, a cashier's check guarantees the recipient gets paid by pulling money directly from the bank instead of someone's account.

Casualty: A loss incurred due to an accident.

Casualty catastrophe: A large loss due to an accident.

Catastrophe futures: A financial instrument purchased by insurance companies as a form of protection against large-scale future losses.

Catastrophe hazard: The danger of a large-scale loss due to a hazard that could affect a large number of insured people; for example, an earthquake.

Catastrophe loss: A difficult-to-predict, severe loss best covered by an insurance company.

Cause of loss form: A form attached to a commercial policy that lists specific causes of loss to be covered by that policy.

Caveat emptor: "Let the buyer beware" in Latin. The buyer purchases property at his or her own risk and shoulders the responsibility of examining it for defects.

Certificate of completion: Paperwork an engineer or architect issues to say a construction project is complete and meets the terms in its blueprint. Signing this document can signal a buyer must now make the final payment.

Certificate of deposit (CD): These are known as time deposits because the depositor agrees to keep money in the bank for a specific amount of time. The bank pays interest to the account holder depending on the amount of money in the CD.

Certificate of deposit index: One way to determine changing interest rates on some adjustable-rate mortgages. It is an annual average of the rate banks pay on CDs.

Certificate of discharge: A written record to show the mortgage is released. It is executed by the mortgagee and given to the mortgagor when the debt secured by a mortgage is satisfied. Sometimes called a release of mortgage.

Certificate of eligibility: A Veterans Administration-issued document that confirms a veteran is able to get a VA loan.

Certificate of insurance: Insurance companies issue this document to confirm they cover someone, and people show the certificates to their lenders to prove they have enough insurance for their property.

Certificate of occupancy (CO): A document saying a structure complies with health requirements and building codes. These certificates come from building agencies or local governments.

Certificate of reasonable value (CRV): A CRV is issued by the Veteran's Administration once the property bought with a VA loan has been appraised.

Certificate of sale: Document one receives when purchasing a building foreclosed for tax reasons. It proves the buyer paid the necessary taxes for the redemption period and claimed the property title afterward.

Certificate of title: An attorney's official opinion on who owns the title to a property or other aspects of its status. The attorney makes this statement after scrutinizing public records.

Certified check: Draws on money in a bank customer's account, not the bank's own funds unlike a cashier's check. These less-secure checks are prohibited in certain real estate transactions.

Certified financial planner: A person who has passed several national exams and been designated by the International Board of Standards and Practices for Certified Financial Planners.

Cestui que vie: Also called the insured or the policyholder. The person whose life dictates the duration of a trust, estate, gift, or insurance contract.

Chain of title: All the times a title has moved from owner to owner until the present. Attorneys use this history to evaluate the title's status.

Change in occupancy or use clause: A change in the use of the premises that increases the possible risk. Once an insurance company receives notice of such a change, they may then increase the premiums or cancel the insurance policy.

Change of beneficiary provision: A provision that permits the insured to change the beneficiary as often as they wish except in policies where the beneficiary is irrevocable. In the case of an irrevocable beneficiary, the beneficiary must provide written consent for a change to be made.

Chattel: Tangible personal property, such as jewelry or clothes.

Circulation factor: Space allowing internal circulation in an office, not part of net square footage.

Civil wrong: An act comprised of two parts. The first, called a tort, is an act against another person or their property. The second is a breach of the terms of a contract.

Claim: A request for disbursement of the benefits promised in the contract.

Claim agent: An agent of the insurance company who has the power to pay the insured for a loss.

Claim department: The insurance company's department that assesses whether or not claims will be paid.

Claim expense: The costs associated with paying a claim, not including the actual cost of the claim.

Claim provision: A clause outlining the process of submitting and administrating claims.

Claim report: A report compiled by an agent detailing the specifics of a claim.

Claimant: The individual requesting payment of a claim.

Claims reserve: Money designated to cover the claims that have occurred but have not yet been settled.

Class: A group of policyholders who have the same characteristics and are grouped together to be rated.

Class "A": High-quality or nicely located property that will bring in a lot of rent money.

Class "B": Desirable property that falls short of bringing in the highest rent price possible.

Class "C": Low-rent property with acceptable living conditions but sparse amenities.

Class rate: A rate for risks grouped into the same class, risks of the same danger.

Clause: A portion of a contract that speaks to a specific issue.

Clear space clause: A clause stating the insured's belongings are to be stored at a certain distance from like-insured or other noninsured belongings.

Clear title: Title free from potential problems or hassles, such as legal encumbrances, defects, and liens.

Clearance letter: The written results of a termite inspection, provided by a licensed inspector. Mortgages backed by the Department of Veterans Affairs or Federal Housing Administration, along with certain other home loans, cannot progress without this letter.

Closing: The end of a sale — when buyer pays the seller; both parties, or their representatives, sign necessary documents, and the buyer receives the title and loan.

Closing costs: Money spent when closing a real estate deal, including fees for appraising property and for the loan and title, but not the actual property.

Closing statement (HUD-1 Settlement Statement): A thorough account of how people spent, gained, and loaned money or started loans; when parties buy and sell real estate.

Cloud on title: Any circumstance or document making it uncertain who holds the title to real estate. Sometimes hard to remove, clouds on title may be cleared up by a suit to quiet title or a quitclaim deed after a title search reveals the cloud.

Cluster housing: Closely grouped homes with tiny yards where residents share a common recreation spot.

CMG plan: A plan implemented to help a borrower pay off a loan early. This mortgage plan is structured similarly to that of a checking account, in which paychecks are direct-deposited into the account, thereby reducing the mortgage payment by that particular amount.

Co-borrower: One or more people who have signed the note and are equally responsible for repaying the loan. *See also "cosigner."*

Co-ownership: When two or more people own a title.

COFI: Acronym for "cost of funds index." It is only one of several indexes used in adjustable rate mortgages to gauge adjustments on the interest rate.

Coinsurance: In property insurance, a formula that outlines the portion of each claim the insurance company will pay.

Coinsurance limit: The amount of coverage mandated by the coinsurance clause in an open stock burglary policy.

Coinsurance penalty: A penalty taken out of the figure the policyholder is given by the insurance company for a property loss. This penalty is assessed due to the insurance company failing to carry enough coverage, as detailed in the coinsurance clause.

Coinsurance percentage: A condition in a property insurance policy that states the policyholder must carry insurance as a percentage of the property's value. Failure to carry this insurance can result in the policyholder being charged the coinsurance penalty.

Coinsurance requirement: The total amount of insurance the policyholder must possess so he or she can be covered for the total amount of a loss and not be charged the coinsurance penalty.

Coinsurer: Under an insurance policy, this is someone who shares in the loss.

Collateral: Something a borrower stands to lose by not paying a debt. The property is collateral in the mortgage loan financing its purchase.

Collateral creditor: A person who has been appointed the rights to a benefit.

Collateralized mortgage obligations (CMO): Real estate mortgages put together and sold in the form of various participating interests.

Collection: When a borrower does not repay a debt, the lender seeks payment and prepares for a possible foreclosure by sending notices to the borrower.

Combined ratio: An expense ratio combined with a loss ratio. In underwriting, if the combined ratio is under 100 percent, a loss occurs. A profit occurs if the combined ratio is more than 100 percent.

Combined single limit: Total liability due to bodily injury and property damage combined as one single sum of coverage.

Commencement of coverage: Date that insurance coverage begins.

Commercial blanket bond: Blanket coverage of employees supplied by the employer. Under this type of coverage, the maximum loss limit is applied to any loss regardless of how many people were involved in the loss.

Commercial credit insurance: Coverage that insures a manufacturing or service organization firm in the case of its debtors defaulting on debts owed.

Commercial forgery policy: Insurance covering a business that unwittingly takes a forged check as payment.

Commercial forms: Insurance against many business risks.

Commercial insurance: Coverage sold by insurance companies with the intent of making a profit.

Commercial insurance company: A company owned by private citizens that sells insurance to make a profit.

Commercial leasehold insurance: Insurance that pays rent if a tenant cannot. Lenders might require businesses in shopping centers to carry this insurance.

Commercial lines: Insurance sold to businesses and other commercial entities.

Commercial mortgage broker: Specializes in brokering mortgages for businesses.

Commercial mortgage lender: Specifically funds mortgage loans for commercial uses.

Commercial mortgage: Money loaned for businesses to buy properties or buildings.

Commercial package policy: Insurance coverage for a commercial organization that covers at least two of the following: commercial property, commercial general liability, business automobile, business crime, boiler and machinery, inland marine, farm owners, and ranch owners.

Commercial property: Slated for businesses, not homes or residential buildings.

Commercial property floater: A way to insure a business that does not operate from one fixed location.

Commercial property policy: Insurance that covers risks associated with operating a business; for example, fire, burglary, or theft.

Commingling: When a real estate agent illegally mixes their own money and a client's in one account instead of keeping the customer's funds in an escrow or trust account.

Commission: Money clients pay brokers for selling or buying property; composed of a certain percent of the property's price.

Commission of authority: The power designated to an agent by an insurance company.

Commissioner of insurance: At the state level, the highest regulator of insurance elected to protect the interests of the policy owner.

Commissioner's values: A list of the securities values published annually by the National Association of Insurance Commissioners. This list is used when documenting the values of the securities owned by the insurance company on its balance sheet.

Commitment fee: Those applying for loans pay this price to lenders, and the lenders agree to follow certain terms on a loan.

Commitment letter: A letter from the lender promising a mortgage at a specific interest rate.

Common (or party) wall: Separates units in a duplex, condominium, or similar building.

Common area assessments (homeowner's association fees): Money condominium owners or planned unit development (PUD) residents give their homeowner's association, which spends it to maintain the building or property.

Common area maintenance (CAM): Fees tenants pay beyond their rent for the upkeep of common facilities, such as parking lots and halls.

Common areas: Used by all condominium residents or unit owners in planned unit developments (PUDs). These spaces are maintained by homeowners' associations using residents' money.

Common law: A system of unwritten laws that has its roots in English customs. Common law changes with the times and is a way of deciding cases based on precedent as opposed to sanctioned law.

Common stock: Publicly traded stock representing a small fraction of a company's equity.

Community property: Purchased by a married couple and, in specific states, owned by both people.

Comparable market analysis: Used to compare properties in the same area to determine property value. Agents use this tool to determine a fair market price for real estate.

Comparable sales (comparables or comps): How much money similar properties nearby sold for. Sellers assume another such property in that area will fetch a comparable price.

Comparative unit method: A way to appraise properties by examining them in chunks of a certain size, such as square feet or acres.

Compensating balances plan: A plan wherein premiums are paid to the insurance company by an insured business. The insurance company then deposits the premium, minus some costs, into a bank account in the insured's name. The insured business can make withdrawals from these funds.

Competent party: Someone who can legally partake in a contract because they are old enough, mentally stable, and not influenced by drugs or alcohol.

Competitive market analysis (CMA): Comparing the price on a seller's home to costs of other houses sold recently that have similar amenities, styles, and locations.

Completion bond: Legal guarantee that a project will be finished as specified.

Compound interest: Additional interest one pays for his or her mortgage, not including the accrued interest.

Comprehensive glass insurance: Insurance that covers glass breaking for almost any reason.

Comprehensive insurance: A general term meaning an insurance policy that covers a large variety of circumstances.

Compulsory insurance: A general term for insurance made mandatory by law.

Concealment: The act of hiding a material fact.

Concessions: Money or other benefits landlords give tenants to encourage them to sign leases.

Concurrent causation: A loss brought about by at least two events. In recent years, concurrent causation has been controversial as one event may be covered but the other not covered.

Condemnation: When the government seizes private property without permission from its owner and renders it public through eminent domain.

Condition: Action that must be completed to have the insurance policy remain valid and for claims to be paid. For example, the policy's premiums must be paid up-to-date.

Condition subsequent: A condition in the policy that will cause the contract to be invalid should a certain event take place.

Conditional: In the insurance contract, the terms that outline the conditions necessary to keep the policy valid.

Conditional commitment: A lender's pledge to loan money if the borrower satisfies specific terms.

Conditional sale: A real estate contract stating the seller owns the property until the buyer fulfills all the contract's conditions.

Conditions for qualification: The duties required of the insured before benefits are paid; for example, submitting an inventory of items lost.

Condominium: Building in which the many residents jointly own common areas and hold titles to private living spaces called units.

Condominium conversion: A rental property that changes from one form of ownership to become a condominium.

Condominium hotel (condotel): Condominium that works as a commercial hotel where people live short term, use a registration desk, and have cleaning, food, and telephone services. Tenants own their living units.

Condominium insurance: Homeowner's insurance covering the insured's property against many perils, including fire, robbery, vandalism, smoke, and explosion.

Condominium owners' association: A group of people who own units in a condominium, manage its common spaces, and enforce its rules.

Confidentiality: The entrustment of proprietary information from one party to another for that party's exclusive use so as not to impart the obtained knowledge to others.

Conforming loan: A mortgage that Freddie Mac or Fannie Mae finds acceptable to purchase.

Consequential loss: An indirect loss caused by the insured not being able to use their property. This type of loss does not happen right away; for example, business interruption. This term can also refer to a loss caused by a hazard the insured is not directly insured for; for example, the spoilage of food due to power outage.

Conservation: An attempt by the insurer to retain current policies by not allowing them to lapse.

Conservator: A person selected by the court or other legal authority to direct an insurance company found to be in danger of failure.

Consideration: A trade of something of value, which becomes the basis of a contract. In the case of insurance, the premium paid by the insured and the future payout of claims by the insurance company is the consideration.

Consolidation: An umbrella company formed with the specific intention of absorbing several other business entities.

Construction documents: Illustrations and notes an engineer or architect makes to specify how a construction project will proceed and what materials it requires.

Construction financing: The method borrowers use to cover the costs of having a house built instead of buying a completely finished house.

Construction insurance: Insurance that covers damage to or destruction of a building while in progress.

Construction loan: A mortgage that covers the costs of building a home. Rather than disburse the entire project at once, construction loans typically disburse payments to the builder of the home in draws as milestones are met on the project. When the construction of the home is complete, permanent mortgage arrangements must be made to pay off the construction loan, but certain ones do not become mortgages.

Consumer price index (CPI): A way to measure inflation based on the prices of things specific populations purchase during certain time periods.

Contents: In personal property insurance, this refers to property that belongs to the insured and is separate from the home; for example, electronics, clothing, and furnishings. The term does not apply to pets, boats, or vehicles. In commercial property insurance, this refers to the business property separate from the business building; for example, office furniture, computers, or machinery.

Contiguous space: Divided spaces over one floor or connecting floors that can combine so a tenant in the building can rent them all simultaneously.

Contingency: Circumstances that must exist for a contract to bind the parties. If a contract is contingent on something that never happens, parties are free from it.

Contingency reserve: A reserve set aside for unforeseen events or damages, found in the insurance company's annual statement.

Contingent fund: A fund set aside for possible losses incurred as a result of a rare event.

Contingent payments: Financial obligations in the future depend on contractual events that take place.

Continuing education requirement: A required minimum amount of insurance-related education that license holders must complete to renew their licenses. Enforced by the state.

Contour map: Displays the physical features of a site — topography — using contour lines for different elevations.

Contract: Legal document binding one or both parties involved to fulfill their promises. If a party breaks its promise in the contract, there is a legal remedy.

Contract carrier: A company that transports the merchandise of certain merchants only as opposed to a carrier who will carry cargo for the general public.

Contract for deed/land contract: Under this contract, a party pays for property in installments. The buyer can live on the property and use it but does not own the title before paying the full price in monthly fees.

Contract for sale: *See "purchase agreement."*

Contract knavery: Putting stipulations or clauses into loan contracts that are disadvantageous to the borrower. The borrower is ignorant of such provisions, and they are sometimes put into place regardless of guarantees and promises of the opposite. Common examples of this include prepayment penalties.

Contract of adhesion: A contract that cannot be bargained over. Insurance contracts are considered contracts of adhesion because the insured cannot negotiate the terms.

Contributing location: One of the four categories of properties covered under business income insurance; a property used to supply equipment or assistance.

Contribution: A term that can have several meanings in the context of insurance. A contribution can be the portion of a loss paid by each insurer when the same loss is covered by two or more insurers. Or the term can mean the portion of a premium paid by the insured. The term can also mean the portion of the loss paid by the insurer under coinsurance.

Control: The power to position insurance where an agent or broker sees fit. This power is granted by the policy owner.

Control provision: A condition that states control is to be given to someone other than the insured. Usually found in contracts for underage people.

Controlled business: The amount of insurance sold by an insurance provider to family and friends. In some states, a limit is placed on this type of business.

Controlled business arrangement: A situation in which consumers are offered a bundle of services, such as real estate agents' aid, mortgage brokerage, and home inspection.

Controlled insurance: Insurance controlled by agent or broker influence instead of by an agreement.

Conventional loan: A long-term loan from a nongovernment lender used by a borrower to buy a house. Conventional loans include fixed-term and fixed-rate mortgages, but not loans backed by the Federal Housing Administration or Department of Veterans Affairs.

Convention blank: A financial statement required in every state. This statement is filed each year in the insurance company's home state, as well as any other state where the insurer possesses a license.

Convention values: The values attributed to the insurer's assets in the convention blank.

Conversion: Assigning property a new use or type of ownership — changing a large house into an apartment complex, for instance.

Conversion option: The choice to switch from an adjustable-rate mortgage to a fixed-rate mortgage at a point throughout the course of its term. Loans that have this option are more likely to have a higher rate than ARMs without the option of conversion.

Convertible ARM: Permits the borrower to switch his or her adjustable-rate mortgage to a fixed-rate mortgage, as long as it occurs within a set amount of time.

Conveyance: The document stating a title passes to a new owner. Also means transference of titles between parties ("closing").

Cooling-off period: Time period when parties can legally abandon a contract and not be bound. For contracts involving private residences, a cooling-off period is mandatory, according to the Truth in Lending Act.

Cooperative (co-op): A complex made up of residents who own shares in the corporation that owns the property. Each resident has rights to one unit in the building.

Cooperative insurance: A policy issued by an association; for example, a trade union or association.

Corporation: Legally considered a single body, registered by the secretary of state. Some features of corporations include unending life, shares that can be traded, central leadership, and limits on their liabilities.

Correspondent: A small lender who is in contact with larger wholesale lenders, to whom he or she delivers loans against price commitments made previously between the two.

COSI: Acronym for "Cost of Savings Index." It is only one of several indexes used in adjustable-rate mortgages to gauge adjustments on the interest rate.

Cosigner: Someone who agrees to pay a debt in the event the borrower cannot. This party or person signs the loan agreement or promissory note alongside the borrower but does not own the title or appear on the deed.

Cost approach appraisal: Approximating a property's value by adding the land's worth to the cost an appraiser says one would pay to replace the building, minus depreciation. This approach does not use prices of nearby homes to estimate a building's value.

Cost-approach land value: The value basic interest in land would carry if the land could be developed for ideal usage.

Cost of funds index (COFI): One way to determine changing interest rates on some adjustable-rate mortgages. COFI expresses the weighted-average cost of savings, borrowings, and advances of financial institutions, in the Federal Home Loan Bank's 11th District.

Cost of living index: Numbers showing how much certain basic commodities cost compared to their prices in a baseline year — how these goods and services have become cheaper or pricier.

Counteroffer: When someone makes an offer and the recipient makes a new offer back while refusing the original.

Countersignature: A licensed agent or representative's signature on a policy.

Countrywide rates: A listing of rates and minimum premiums for each major division in the Commercial Lines Manual.

Countrywide rules: A listing of rules and rating factors for each major division in the Commercial Lines Manual.

Courier fee: Cost for delivering documents to all those involved in a real estate deal, which they pay when the transaction closes.

Courtesy to brokers: Act of splitting pay between cooperating brokers and listing brokers.

Covenant against encumbrances: An agreement, promise, or contract that shows there are no encumbrances against the land outlined in a deed or other recorded means of communication. An encumbrance is a claim by another person against the land. Leases, mortgages, liens, unpaid taxes, or easements are examples of encumbrances.

Covenant: An agreement binding at least two parties, it appears in documents such as leases, deed contracts, and mortgages. Parties in the covenant promise to act certain ways toward a property.

Covenant not to compete (noncompete clause or noncompete covenant): One party promises in writing not to make or distribute the same products as the other party within a certain area.

Covenant of quiet enjoyment: An agreement, promise, or contract that shows the grantee to a deed or other conveyance will have the land in peace, with no outside disturbances from another person who might have adverse claims on the land.

Covenant of right to convey: An agreement, promise, or contract that shows the grantor may transfer the title of the real estate.

Covenant of seisin: An agreement, promise, or contract that shows the grantor holds quantity and equality of the land described in the deed or other recorded means of communication.

Cover: An insurance contract. This term can also be used to describe the act of incorporating something in a contract of insurance; for example, a newly acquired vehicle. It can also mean to provide coverage to an insured person.

Cover note: A note written by an agent notifying the insured that his or her coverage has taken effect. Comparable to a binder but not issued by a company like a binder.

Coverage: The extent of the coverage supplied by the insurance contract.

Coverage part: Any of the parts of commercial coverage that may be included with a commercial contract. These may be issued as a policy or attached to part of a policy.

Covered loss: Any type of loss the insurer will pay under a policy. This can include death, injury, property damage or loss, or automobile collision.

Covered person: Any person covered under an insurance contract.

Creative financing: A nontraditional mortgage from a third-party lender, such as a balloon payment.

Credit: Borrowing money to purchase something valuable and agreeing to repay the lender afterward.

Credit bureau: Company that creates and maintains the credit reports of people in the United States. The three major credit-reporting bureaus are Equifax, TransUnion, and Experion. Creditors report information on borrowers to the bureau. This information is used to create a credit report.

Credit card insurance: Coverage usually provided under a homeowner's policy that covers the insured in the event of fraudulent credit card use.

Credit history: A record of someone's debts, past and present, and how reliably the person settled them.

Credit rating: Number describing how much someone deserves a loan. It is determined from current finances and credit history.

Credit report: A record of someone's prior residences, jobs, and credit used to determine if the person is worthy of further credit.

Credit repository: Companies that collect, update, and store financial and public information about the payment records of individuals who have applied for credit.

Credit score (credit risk score or FICO score): A calculated summary of the data on someone's credit report.

Credit tenant: A tenant with the size and financial strength worthy enough of being rated as an investment grade by one of three major credit agencies: Fitch, Moody's, or Standard & Poor's. An investment grade rating is seen as a good sign that the tenant will be able to pay rent, even in economic downturns or specific market slumps.

Creditor: A party owed money.

Criticism: An auditor's submission of a modification to an insurer.

Cromie rule: A technique for apportioning loss under policies with nonidentical coverage.

Crop insurance: Covers loss of crops due to weather conditions; for example, rain or hail.

Cumulative interest: Adding up all interest payments to the present date or over the loan's entire term or life. Cumulative interest is added to the original amount invested, so it does not include initial cash payments, nor is it adjusted for money's time value.

Curb appeal: A property or home's good looks, as noted by viewers on its street.

Current value: The financial worth at the appraisal time.

Currently insured status: Under old age, survivors, and disability health insurance, this is a status with fewer requirements to obtain than a status of fully insured. This status also allows the insured's dependents to survivor benefits in the case of the insured's death.

D

Daily report: A condensed statement containing relevant policy information sent to the insurer, the agent, and select others. This is usually the top page of the policy.

Damages: Amount of money someone gets through legal means because someone harmed them in any fashion. This includes damaging an owner's building.

Data processing coverage: This type of coverage protects the insured against a data processing system failure. The insured is also covered for the cost of restoring the system.

Date of issue: The date the policy was created by the insurer. This can be a different date than the effective date.

DBA: Doing Business As. Used to note someone's invented business name or trade name but not meant to deceive clients.

Deadbeat: Someone who borrows money and does not pay.

Deal flow: A steady flow of potential business acquisitions in such a quantity that allows you to select the ones that meet your desired criteria.

Debit: The amount of premiums outstanding and business to be collected by debit or home service agents. This can also refer to the area these customers live in.

Debris removal clause: In a property insurance contract, this clause allows the insured to be reimbursed for expenses associated with the cleanup of debris created by an insured loss.

Debt capital: The amount of a debt a REIT carries on a balance sheet, excluding equity capital, such as a common or preferred stock. This can include short-term variable-rate debt, secured or unsecured debt, and long-term, fixed-rate mortgage debt.

Debt consolidation: When a borrower takes a loan against property and uses the money to pay off other debts, such as loans and credit cards. The borrower's debts are consolidated into one payment, generally with a lower interest rate.

Debt elimination: Deceptive promises devised to relieve borrowers of their money. These scams make claims of totally eliminating one's mortgage debt.

Debt financing: Borrowing money, usually in the form of a loan, and being charged a fee for its use, usually in the form of interest.

Debt service: Total money one needs to pay all the principal and interest of a loan for a certain amount of time.

Debtaholic: A person who borrows money and struggles to control the amount of debt incurred. The only way for debtaholics to handle debt is to completely stay away from temptations, such as credit cards.

Debt-to-equity ratio: How much unpaid mortgage a property has compared with its equity. The ratio would be 2:1 if a property had $100,000 of unpaid debt and $50,000 of equity.

Debt-to-income ratio: The percent of monthly income someone spends repaying a debt. To calculate, divide the monthly money paid toward the debt by that month's gross income.

Decedent: Synonym for deceased.

Declaration: A legal term for a written declaration, made under oath, of what the individual knows to be factual information. In liability or property insurance, a declaration is the part of the contract that contains basic information; for example, the insured's contact information or the address of the property.

Declaration of restrictions: Rules people must follow if they live in a given condominium or subdivision.

Declination: When the insurer declines an application for coverage.

Decree: A government- or court-issued order.

Deductible: A fraction of the insured loss, which must be paid by the insured before the insurer will pay.

Deductible clause: A clause in the contract that states the deductible amount.

Deed: This document legally transfers property to a new owner. That buyer gets the deed after negotiating with and paying the seller.

Deed in lieu of foreclosure: Returning one's property to a lender without foreclosure proceedings to avoid their negative effects and costs.

Deed of trust: A relationship in which a land trust gives the trustee authority to mortgage, subdivide, or sell real estate. How the trustee can use these powers is up to the beneficiary who provided the trust. A deed in trust is also a loan term stating that if a debtor defaults, the lender can foreclose on the property.

Deed restrictions: Restrictions given in a deed on how property can be used. They can limit what kind of new structures people can build there or what activities or objects are allowed on the property.

Defamation: A legal term for a statement meant to damage a person's reputation or business.

Default: A borrower defaults by failing to pay their mortgage or perform some other obligatory duty.

Deferred maintenance: Appraisers using this term refer to property defects the owner has not repaired, such as chipped paint or broken windows.

Deferred payment method: Strategy of delaying the date when someone will begin repaying a loan.

Deficiency judgment: A borrower is charged with a deficiency judgment when his or her property is foreclosed, but selling it does not produce enough money to cover the remaining unpaid mortgage.

Degree of risk: The uncertainty present in a particular situation.

Delayed exchange: When a party trades property for a second piece of real estate but does not receive it right away. This delay lets that party defer all taxable gains on the first piece of property.

Delinquency: When a borrower misses mortgage payments. If continued, it brings foreclosure.

Delivery: Someone's real estate or other possession passing to a different person.

Demand clause: A clause in the note that states the note is payable on demand of the holder.

Demand loan: In this type of loan, lenders can call for buyers to fully repay them for whatever reason, anytime.

Demising wall: Separates a tenant's unit from a hall, other common area, or another tenant's living space.

Demolition clause: A clause that prohibits accountability for costs that result from demolishing property that is not damaged. This is frequently done due to building ordinances that require demolition of structures after they suffer a certain amount of damage.

Demolition insurance: Insurance that covers the charges stemming from demolition that is not covered under a demolition clause.

Density: How concentrated the buildings are in a certain spot, buildings per unit area.

Density zoning: These zoning ordinances limit the number of houses each acre of land can contain, on average, for a certain area.

Department of Housing and Urban Development (HUD): This government agency works to provide clean and safe living spaces without discrimination. It executes plans for community development and federal housing.

Dependent: A person dependent on another person for support and to maintain his or her lifestyle.

Dependent properties: Properties that contribute to the insured's income but are not owned or operated by the insured; for example, customers.

Deposit (earnest money): Money one pays when offering to buy a property.

Deposit or provisional premium: A premium amount derived from an approximate value of the final premium. This premium is paid at the start of the policy.

Depreciation: Appraisers use this term to mean lessened value of a property because it grows old, obsolete, or has other defects. For real estate investors, this term means a tax deduction taken while owning income property.

Depreciation insurance: Insurance that provides for the replacement value of property that has been damaged. Depreciation is not subtracted from the value of the item.

Description: *See "land description."*

Desecuritization: Flip-flopping the securitization system by making singular loans out of a security.

Design-build: Situation in which one person manages the construction and design of a building. *Also see "build to suit."*

Designated agent: Someone who holds a real estate license and has authority to be another's agent, backed by a broker.

Development loan (construction loan): Borrowed funds to buy real estate, prepare it for construction, and erect buildings.

Deviated rate: A rate offered by a company that usually follows the rates recommended by a lawyer, which is lower than the recommended rate in that area.

Deviation: A rate different from the manual rate.

Devise: Act of awarding someone real estate through a will. The devisor, or donor, leaves the property to the devisee.

Difference in conditions: A contract separate from the existing policy that complements or increases the property insurance, so the property is now protected from all risks, minus some exclusions.

Dilution: An investor's percentage of ownership is reduced by additional stock issued during future rounds of financing.

Direct loss: Damage that directly occurs as a result of a particular hazard; for example, flood damage.

Direct sales comparisons approach (market comparison approach): An appraiser places a value on property by examining the prices on recently purchased estates nearby with similar qualities.

Direct selling system: A system for selling insurance in which the insurer sells directly to the insured via its employees. This includes insurance sold through mail order services.

Direct writer: An insurer who uses the direct selling system, or the exclusive agency system, to sell his or her products.

Direct written premium: The amount of the premiums that have been collected before deducting any premiums sent to reinsurers.

Director of insurance: A term used for the leader of the department of insurance in some states.

Disability: A medical condition or psychological affliction that limits the individual's capability to engage in everyday activities. This may be a temporary or permanent circumstance.

Disappearing deductible: A deductible that progressively fades away as the loss amount grows bigger. A deductible of $50 to $500 is progressively reduced, and losses that equal $500 are fully covered.

Disaster myopia: Lenders' habits of overlooking possible shocks that could produce hefty losses if a long time has gone by since a shock last took place.

Disbursement: Money someone loans, invests, or otherwise pays out.

Discharge in bankruptcy: Occurs when a bankrupt party is freed from the debts they were assigned during bankruptcy proceedings.

Disclaimer: Statement that someone is surrendering property they owned or washing their hands of responsibilities.

Disclosure: A document listing all the relevant positive and negative information about a piece of real estate.

Disclosure authorization form: A form that permits the disclosure of private information acquired during an insurance-related business. By law, the form must disclose what information will be collected and whom it will be shared with.

Discount broker: A broker whose fees are lower than most. These costs might be a flat rate instead of a percentage of the sale.

Discount points: Fees the lender can charge with lower interest rates than typical loan payments. Discount points represent different loan percentages, with one point equaling one percent of the loaned money.

Discount rate: The interest rate the Federal Reserve charges for loaning money to commercial banks.

Discounted cash flow (DCF): A measurement designed to find the value of a REIT by calculating the current value of future distributable income. By looking at this measurement in conjunction with a REIT's net present value per share, investors can gauge whether the current share price is undervaluing or overvaluing a REIT.

Discounted properties: Properties priced below the appraised value.

Discounted value table: A table that gives the value of dollars payable at certain times in the future. The table shows values at present and discounted for different interest rates.

Discretionary ARM: A type of adjustable rate mortgage that only requires the lender to provide prior notice before he or she makes adjustments to the interest rate. Discretionary ARMs are not found in the United States, only abroad.

Discrimination: Prohibited by law, discrimination is the refusal to insure certain people who have the same characteristics as others who have been insured.

Divided cover: Insuring a person or object with more than one insurer.

Dividend: When an insurer returns a portion of the premium paid by an insured for a policy. Or, a part of a surplus paid to each stockholder in a company.

Dividend reinvestment programs (DRIP): A program allowing REITs to directly offer an investor the opportunity to pass the quarterly dividend back to the company. The investment refund from the dividends can then be used for price appreciation and compounding without incurring brokerage fees. DRIPs allow investors to take advantage of dollar cost averaging with income — the corporate dividends — the company is paying out. This way, an investor gets the return of the yield, as well as the potential of stock gains. An investor must still pay taxes on a DRIP.

Divisible contract clause: A clause stating coverage will not be voided at all locations if the conditions of the policy are violated at another location.

Documentary tax stamps: Stamps attached to a deed, which represent the tax amount paid during the transfer of ownership on the property.

Documentation requirements: Specifics set forth by the lender that establish how a loan applicant's information on earnings and assets must be given, as well as how the lender will use that information.

Dollar limit: A limit on coverage in a homeowner's policy. This is usually listed in the Coverage C section of the policy.

Domestic insurer: An insurance company founded in the same state in which it opened.

Down payment: The sum of money the buyer gives the lender or seller in order to purchase the property; the balance of the selling price is then considered the mortgage.

DownREIT: A REIT that owns and operates properties besides its interest in a separate controlled partnership. This is similar to an UPREIT (*see "umbrella partnership"*) with the main difference being a downREIT is normally formed after the REIT has become a public entity.

Dry closing: Both parties have made their agreement but have not exchanged money or documents. The escrow will finish the closing.

Dry mortgage (nonrecourse loan): A mortgage for which the borrower pledges property for collateral but stands to lose nothing else to the lender and is not personally liable.

Dual apper: A borrower who utilizes two loan providers through which to give loan applications.

Dual index mortgage: A type of mortgage that stipulates the changing of the interest rate depending on an interest rate index. The mortgage's monthly payment is also adjusted based on salary index and wage.

Dual life stock company: A life insurance company that issues participating and nonparticipating policy contracts.

Due diligence: Actions by someone looking to purchase real estate — checking the property for defects or hazards and verifying a seller represents it.

Due on sale clause: A mortgage provision stating if the borrower sells the property the loan covers, they must immediately pay the rest of the mortgage debt to the lender.

Dun and Bradstreet, Inc.: A company that aids insurers in underwriting possible insureds by providing the insurer with financial information.

Duress: Circumstance where someone is illegally coerced or threatened to act unwillingly. If someone joins a contract under duress, it can be canceled.

Dwelling forms: A policy that covers a building in which people reside and personal possessions kept within.

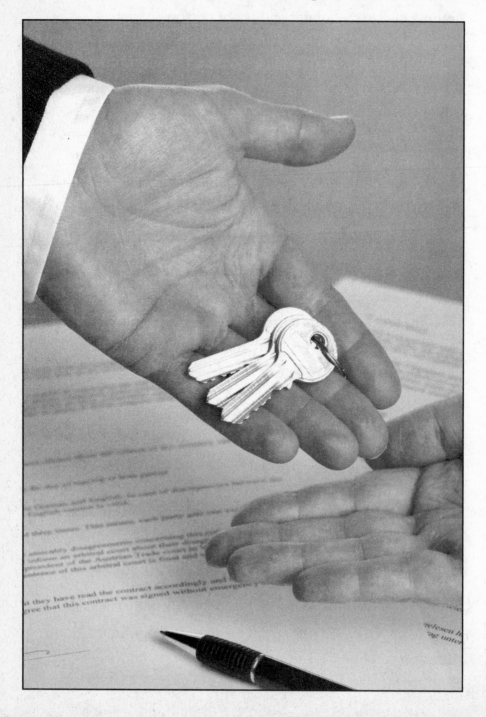

E

Earned income: The money a person earns from working at a job.

Earned premium: Part of a premium exhausted during the term of the policy.

Earnest money: Money a buyer deposits under a contract and loses if he backs out of purchasing the property. But, if he buys the real estate, the money goes toward that sale.

Earn-outs: Part of the purchase price that depends on a future performance variable, such as sales or profits.

Earnings insurance: Business interruption insurance without a coinsurance clause. This coverage is meant for smaller risks.

Earth movement: A danger often excluded from homeowner's policies; for example, an earthquake, mudslide, or the sinking of the earth. Earth movement is also often excluded from commercial property policies.

Earthquake insurance: Insurance that covers loss of property or damage due to an earthquake.

Easement: A party's right to use a portion of a property it does not own for defined purposes, such as accommodating telephone or power lines.

Easement in gross: An easement tied personally to its owner, not meant to benefit any of the owner's land. One example involves someone granting another person rights to access part of his or her property for life.

EBIT: The acronym for "earnings before interest and taxes."

EBITDA: Earnings before interest, taxes, depreciation, and amortization. *See also "net operating income."*

EBITDA – CAP-X: This is a more practical assessment of earnings than with EBITDA. It stands for EBITDA minus capital expenditures.

Economic life: How many years an improvement will continue giving property value.

Economic obsolescence (environmental or external obsolescence): Decrease in a property's value as changes to surrounding areas render it obsolete or less desirable.

Effective age: An assessment of a building's condition an appraiser presents.

Effective date: Date when securities can initiate once a registration statement takes effect.

Effective gross income: How much gross income a property can bring in after subtracting an allowance for vacancy and collection.

Effective rate: Can be used two ways. One is an interest cost identical to APR determined over a time period specified by the borrower. Most times it is a rate adjusted for intra-year compounding, such as rate per month; for example, .5 percent per month if quoted 6 percent annually. In this case, the return is 6.17 percent annually. This is the effective rate.

Efficiency unit: Small, one-room living space in a building housing several families. These units might lack full bathroom and kitchen facilities.

Egress: Way to exit a property via a public road or other means.

Electrical or electrical apparatus exemption clause: A clause that says damage to appliances stemming from electrical currents is only covered if a fire starts.

Electronic data processing coverage: Insurance that covers computers, data systems, and income lost due to loss of electronic data processing capability.

Elevation drawing: An illustration showing property from the front, side, or back to demonstrate how it is situated without including perspective.

Elevator collision coverage: Insurance that covers damage to elevators brought about by elevator collision. This insurance also covers personal possessions and the building that houses the elevator. This coverage is often included in business liability insurance policies.

Eminent domain: Government ability to buy property at market price and render it public.

Encroachment: Part of a building or other structure illegally intruding on another's land or an alley or street. Encroachment includes any upgrade or improvement extending onto someone else's lot unlawfully.

Encumbrance: Anything that diminishes a property's worth or makes it less useful or enjoyable. Examples include taxes, mortgages, easements, judgment liens, and rules restricting how the property is used.

Endorsement: Signing the back of a check one pays. Also, endorsement means supporting a statement or making it more credible.

Endorsement extending period of indemnity: An attachment to a business interruption policy extending the coverage period to include the time after the business reopens but does not yet do the amount of business it did before the interruption.

Enterprise value: Market value of equity plus interest-bearing debt.

Entitlement: Being owed something with legal backing. Entitlement also refers to protection of the lender by the Department of Veterans Affairs in case the veteran cannot pay.

Entity: A legally recognized corporation or person.

Entrepreneur: Taken from the German word "unternehmer," referring to a person who owns and runs his or her own business.

Environmental audit: Examination of a property for hazards.

Environmental impact statement: Document stating the negative effects of a major project on the environment, as required by law.

Environmental Protection Agency (EPA): Federal agency that works to prevent pollution and enforces national laws against it.

Equal Credit Opportunity Act (ECOA): A law that dictates credit be equally available to all applicants. Discrimination based on sex, sexual orientation, race, national origin, religion, age, marital status, or income is not tolerated.

Equalization factor: A number by which one multiplies a property's value to align it with state tax assessments. This adjusted value provides a basis for the ad valorem tax.

Equipment breakdown insurance: Commercial insurance covering any loss caused by the breakdown of machinery or other equipment.

Equipment floater: Coverage against specific types of damage on different types of equipment.

Equitization: This is the process of how real estate or other tangible assets are divided among several investors and placed into publicly traded stock. In some accounting principles, it also allows the parent company of the entity to calculate the net income of subsidiaries on a monthly basis and then increase the investment, if necessary, before consolidating properties and assets.

Equity: The difference between the present market value of the home and the amount owed. If the home is worth $200,000 and the borrower owes $125,000 on a mortgage, the equity is $75,000.

Equity buildup: Equity gradually accumulating as the borrower repays the loan.

Equity grabbing: A thievish type of lending in which the lender wants the borrower to default so he or she can seize equity from the borrower.

Equity mortgage: *See "home equity line" and "home equity loan."*

Equity of redemption: The owner's right to recover property before the foreclosure sale, providing he or she comes up with enough money for loan payments and real estate taxes.

Equity REIT: A REIT that owns or has a financial or equity interest in a variety of real estate.

Equity sharing: A form of collective partnership between an owner/investor and an owner/occupant. The investor takes deductions in the loss of value for his or her share of the ownership. For the occupant, a part of his or her monthly payment is treated as rent. Additionally, the occupant acquires part of the tax write-offs for interest and taxes. Both owners equally divide the profit once the property is sold. Compare to joint ownership.

Errors and omissions insurance: Protects against errors made by either a builder or architect.

Escalation clause: A lease term stating the landlord can raise rent if his or her own expenses grow.

Escalator clause: A lease term requiring tenants to pay higher rent as costs increase.

Escape clause: Releases parties from the sale contract if something expected does not happen; for instance, if a buyer cannot secure a loan to purchase the property.

Escrow abuse: The habit some lenders get into to produce considerably more income from unsuspecting borrowers by inappropriately using their escrow accounts.

Escrow account (impound account): Used by mortgage lenders and servicing businesses to store money that will pay real estate taxes, homeowner's insurance, and other items.

Escrow agent (escrow company): A third party who neutrally ensures those having a real estate transaction meet the necessary conditions, such as putting valuables in an escrow account before any money or property changes hands.

Escrow: Closing of a deal by an escrow agent — a neutral third party. Escrows are also sums of money or valuable possessions passed to a third party, who delivers them when certain conditions are met.

Escrow disbursement: Paying out the money from an escrow account for property expenses due, such as mortgage insurance or taxes.

Estate: Someone's property and all other assets after he or she dies.

Estate in land: Details on how much interest someone holds in real estate and the nature of that interest.

Estate plan: A will and other provisions for the distribution of one's estate upon death or disability.

Estimated closing costs: Approximately how much it costs for a real estate sale to occur.

Estimated premium: A projected premium amount that is later adjusted.

Ethics: Moral code that guides professional behavior.

Eviction: Removal of a property's occupant by law.

Evidence clause: A clause that obligates the insured to assist the adjuster in determining the legitimacy of a claim by producing documents and being examined.

Evidence of title: A certificate of title or other proof that one owns a property. Examples include title insurance, a Torrens registration certificate, or an abstract of title along with a lawyer's opinion.

Ex gratia payment: Compensation from the insurer not required by the contract. The insurer may occasionally pay a claim, though he or she is not liable as an act of goodwill.

Examination: An evaluation conducted by the state insurance department of an insurance company.

Examination of title: An inquiry and report revealing who has owned a property through its history, performed by title companies.

Examiner: A general term for a state insurance department employee sent to audit an insurer.

Exception: Something an insurance policy does not cover.

Excess insurance: A secondary coverage that pays in excess of the primary policy. Excess insurance does not pay unless the amount lost exceeds a specified amount.

Excess line broker: A broker who has a license to deal with insurers not admitted in his or her state.

Exchange: A swap of similar property. For example, trading two pieces of real estate.

Exclusion: A clause in the contract denying coverage for specific hazards, people, or property.

Exclusion rider: An attachment to a policy that eliminates coverage for certain hazards.

Exclusive agency listing: When an owner exclusively contracts and pays a real estate broker to sell a property under the owner's specific terms during a certain time period. The owner can still sell the property himself without paying the broker if he finds a buyer the broker has not claimed or approached.

Exclusive agency system: A system of insurance sales, where agents only provide business to one company or give the right of first refusal to a certain company.

Executed contract: An accord for which each party has completed its duty.

Executor (executrix for females): The person a will names to manage an estate.

Exhibit: A secondary document used in support of a different, main document.

Exhibitions insurance: Coverage that protects an individual who displays his or her property at public exhibitions against damage to the property.

Exit strategy: For investors, how and when they will receive the return on their investment. For founders, how and when they will compensate themselves for making the business a success, usually either by selling the business or by selling the stock they have in the business.

Expansion option: A lease provision allowing a tenant to lease bordering areas and expand his or her rented space after a certain amount of time. This provision shows up in commercial leases.

Expediting expenses: Costs sustained by a business attempting to hurry a reopening after damage.

Expense allowance: Payment made to an insurance agent in addition to set commissions.

Expense constant: A charge added to the premium amount. Most often, this is done to worker's compensation policies or other small policies that have low premiums. The cost of servicing these policies is too much to recoup on premiums alone.

Expense loading: An amount added to the rate to cover expenses.

Expense ratio: The portion of the premium dedicated to paying the insurer's expenses. Losses are not included.

Expense reimbursement allowance: Additional payment made to an insurance agent to set commissions.

Expense reserve: The liability to the insurer for expenses incurred but not paid.

Expenses: All the costs of doing business, including desk fees, agent fees for advertising, and other factors considered to be expenses for real estate agents.

Experience: The record of loss belonging to an agent, insured, or another category. This term can also mean a statistic made up of the ratio of losses to premiums.

Experience modification: A premium amount increase or decrease caused by the use of an experience-rating plan.

Experience rating: A way of adjusting premium amounts based on previous experiences for that specific risk instead of being based on loss experience for all risks.

Expiration: The termination date listed in a contract.

Expiration card: A method of noting the expiration date of a policy. The agent or salesperson may use this to remind him or herself of which policies will be up for renewal soon.

Expiration file: A notation of the day on which policies expire, kept by agents or salespeople.

Expiration notice: Notice given to the insured of the upcoming expiration of the insurance.

Expired: Past real estate listings in the MLS that did not sell during the designated time allotted for the listing agreement.

Explosion insurance: Insurance that covers loss of property because of explosion. This coverage does not apply to explosion of steam boilers and other pressurized instruments.

Exposure: Being in a situation that makes it possible to suffer a loss. This term can also mean the chance of a loss happening due to the area around the insured. Another possible meaning of this term is in the context of an area around the insured that results in a loss to the insured.

Exposure units: People or possessions that may be subject to a loss that can be given a cash value. This term can also refer to the premium base.

Express agreement: A written or verbal contract allowing parties to declare their intentions and contract terms in speech.

Express authority: Authority granted to the agent by the insurer, by way of the agency agreement.

Extended coverage: Extra insurance against problems that homeowner's policies do not typically cover or for uncommon hazards a property faces.

Extended period of indemnity: Coverage that extends the existing lost income coverage for a certain time after business resumes.

Extender clause: This rarely used clause makes a listing agreement renewable automatically until involved parties decide to end it.

Extension: When both parties agree to lengthen a time period given by a contract.

Extra expense coverage form: A form that covers added costs to a business that needs to remain open after a property loss.

Extra expense insurance: A form that provides compensation for costs associated with the operation of a business damaged by a hazard listed in the insurance contract. This form is usually used by businesses that cannot afford to close for fear of losing customers.

Extra premium: A charge added to a premium because the regular premium rate does not take into account certain hazards.

Extra premium removal: Elimination of an extra premium because the hazard necessitating it no longer exists.

F

Face amount: The total amount of coverage provided by an insurance contract, as stated on the face.

Fair Access to Insurance Requirements (FAIR) Plan: A plan instituted by the federal government, similar to stop loss reinsurance. If a property owner, commercial or residential, cannot obtain property insurance, he or she can apply to an insurance agent who works for a FAIR Plan insurer. Should the property be found acceptable, he or she will be insured. If not, the company will suggest improvements to the property and will insure it after the improvements are made.

Fair Credit Reporting Act (FCRA): Federal laws governing the procedures credit reporting agencies use.

Fair Housing Act: Federal legislation stating someone providing housing cannot discriminate against people because of religion, gender, disability, appearance, race, nationality, or familial status.

Fair market value: Price determined by how much a buyer will agree to pay and how little a seller will accept. In a competitive market, properties would sell at certain times for market value.

Fair rental value coverage: Coverage that protects the rental income an insured receives from an insured building. If a building usually rented to others is damaged by a hazard named in the policy, this coverage will pay the rental value.

Fallen building clause: A clause in a property insurance policy stipulating that if a portion of the building collapses for any reason other than fire or explosion, the fire insurance is voided.

Fallout: Borrowers' withdrawn loan applications. This sometimes occurs when a borrower has found a better deal elsewhere.

FAMEMP: Stands for "fully amortizing mortgage with equal monthly payments."

Fannie Mae Community Home Buyer's Program: In this type of community lending meant to help low- to medium-income families buy homes, Fannie Mae and mortgage insurers provide flexible guidelines for participating lenders to underwrite loans and decide who has enough credit to receive them.

Fannie Mae: *See "Federal National Mortgage Association."*

Farm coverage part: A part offered in the commercial package policy that covers farmland, equipment, and livestock.

Farm personal property: Property not covered under farm property coverage; for example, livestock, grain, and harvest equipment.

Farm property coverage form: Farm coverage for the residence, household property, and farm buildings.

Farmer's Home Administration (FMHA): Part of the U.S. Department of Agriculture, this agency gives farmers and rural people access to credit.

Farmer's/ranch owner's policy: Comparative to homeowner's insurance, adapted to cover a farm. This is a package policy that covers farm residences and the property within — barns, stables, and other farm buildings.

Feasibility study: Determines how well a proposed development will achieve an investor's goals. It appraises income, expenses, and how the property can be used or designed to greatest effect.

Federal Deposit Insurance Corporation (FDIC): An independent part of the U.S. government, this agency insures commercial banks' deposits.

Federal Emergency Management Agency (FEMA): Provides flood insurance for property owners at risk and performs other functions.

Federal estate tax: A federal estate tax on the estate of a deceased person.

Federal Home Loan Mortgage Corporation (Freddie Mac):
Government agency that buys home mortgages.

Federal Housing Administration (FHA): This government
agency works to make housing available by providing loan
programs, as well as guarantee and insurance programs
for loans.

Federal Insurance Administration: A division of the United
States Department of Housing and Urban Development that
administers food plans, FAIR plans, and federal crime insurance.

Federal Insurance Contributions Act (FICA): A law that
mandates payroll taxes, which help to fund security and
Medicare benefits. Under FICA, the employer and the employee
make equal contributions through their taxes. The employer
pays taxes on payroll, while the workers pay taxes on their
salaries or wages earned.

Federal National Mortgage Association (FNMA): This
shareholder-owned company is nicknamed Fannie Mae. It is
congressionally chartered and leads the nation in supplying
mortgage funds. Fannie Mae purchases lenders' mortgages and
sells them as securities in secondary mortgage markets.

Federal Reserve System: Supplies the country with money and
sets interest rates, acting as nation's primary banking system.

Federal tax lien: A debt set against a piece of real estate when someone neglects to pay federal taxes. The Internal Revenue Service uses this lien to encourage the owner to pay income taxes.

Fee appraiser (independent fee appraiser or review appraiser): Someone a prospective property buyer pays to appraise real estate.

Fee for service: Money a consumer pays someone holding a real estate license for services.

Fee simple: The greatest interest in real estate that laws recognize. It entitles the interested party to all possible property rights.

Fee simple estate: The highest form of real estate ownership recognized by law, in which the owner can enjoy the property to its fullest extent and is only limited by zoning laws or other similar restrictions. The fee simple estate has unlimited duration and can be passed on to heirs. In relation to property in a condominium, the owner of a unit is owner only of his or her portion of the building and jointly owns the land and common areas of the property with other tenants.

Feudal system: In this system, a sovereign ruler controls all rights and allows people to own property only during life. When someone dies, the king or other ruler gets the title back. Pre-colonial England used a feudal system.

FHA loan: Given by a lender approved by the Federal Housing Administration. The FHA insures this loan.

FICO score: The FICO score is a credit score. These are used by mortgage lenders to predict the borrower's ability and willingness to pay debts. FICO is an acronym for the Fair Isaac Corporation, which calculates the credit scores in the United States.

Fictitious groups: Groups created with the intention of purchasing insurance. These groups are barred by law from being insured.

Fiduciary: A person charged with the money or property of another, which is being held in trust. The fiduciary is legally obligated to act ethically in this position.

Fiduciary relationship: A confident and trusting relationship between principal and agent or another two parties.

Field: A category of insurance; for example, the health insurance field. This term can also refer to a specific region being served by an agent or insurer.

Field force: The agents and supervisors working for an insurance company in local offices.

Filled land: Land artificially raised with piled rocks, gravel, or dirt. If a property has filled land, sellers disclose that fact to buyers.

Final inspection: The last inspection of the property being purchased prior to closing. This inspection is done to determine the condition of the property and ensure the property is in the same condition as at the time of the agreement of sale.

Financing: The money a lender is loaning to the borrower for a set number of years with a repayment plan.

Financing charge: Interest charged to a borrower by a lender.

Financing gap: Portion of a property's price the buyer cannot afford. For example, a buyer might have funds and loans covering 90 percent of a $100,000 real estate sale, which leaves a $10,000 gap.

Financing points: Adding points, or fees, to the amount of the loan taken out.

Finder's fee: A commission for merely identifying and introducing a buyer to the seller; does not include other services such as valuing, structuring, and negotiating.

Fine print: Small-size type in a contract that is purported to contain omissions, exemptions, and coverage limits. State laws largely prohibit printing exclusions in smaller font than that used for the rest of the contract. Laws also mandate the size of font used in contracts.

Fire: Combustion intense enough to result in a flame or a glow. Only hostile fires, which are unintentional or have grown outside the intended area, are covered by property insurance.

Fire, Casualty, and Surety (FC&S) bulletins: Bulletins from the National Underwriter Company that detail coverage and underwriting for various types of policies within the categories of insurance.

Fire department service clause: A clause within a fire insurance contract that provides that the insured will be reimbursed for any expenses caused by the fire department attempting to save their property.

Fire insurance: Covers property lost or damaged in a fire. It can include related water or smoke damage.

Fire legal liability: A policy that covers the insured in case of liability due to negligence that causes fire to spread to another's property.

Fire loss insurance: The first policy that claims are submitted to for a loss before any other policy that covers the same peril. This term can also mean a policy written for an amount that covers the anticipated loss during the policy term.

Fire maps: Maps that show all fire insurance written by all insurers. These maps are a visual representation of the insured's covered risks in the area, which helps the insurer to avoid catastrophic losses.

Fire wall: Made of fire-resistant substances meant to slow spreading flames.

Firm commitment: In this document, a lender agrees to loan a borrower money needed to buy property.

First mortgage: A property's original mortgage, which must be paid before any others. When a property has more than one lien, the first mortgage is most important, and it is the earliest debt settled for a foreclosed property.

First named insured: The first person listed on a commercial insurance policy.

First party insurance: Insurance that covers the policyholder's property or self.

Fiscal year: The 12-month calendar of financial reports, typically starting the first day of January.

Fixed costs and fixed expenses: Fees that do not change with productivity, sales success, or a property's occupants. Unlike utility bills, which depend on how much water or electricity one uses, fixed costs such as fixed-rate mortgage payments remain steady.

Fixed-markup UML: An upfront mortgage lender who reveals his or her price markup and wholesale prices.

Fixed-rate mortgage: A constant interest rate on a home loan.

Fixture: A possession one fixes permanently to a property, making it part of the real estate.

Flag lot: Skirting a subdivision's rules by dividing property into distinct parcels.

Flat: An apartment on one story only.

Flat cancellation: A policy cancelled on the effective date. Usually, no premiums have been paid.

Flat commission: A standard commission paid to the insurance agent no matter what kind of policy has been sold.

Flat deductible: A particular sum deducted from every loss or claim filed.

Flex space: A structure with offices or showrooms that also contains space for factory work, laboratories, storage and other purposes. The arrangement of these different spaces can change.

Flexible payment mortgage (adjustable-rate mortgage):
A variable interest rate on a home loan that changes while allowing the borrower to repay the debt.

Flip: To profit by purchasing and quickly reselling property.

Float: When the borrower has been approved for a mortgage but is waiting for paperwork to be completed and closing scheduled, the borrower may choose to either float or lock the interest rate. Floating the rate means the borrower is waiting to see if the rate will get lower in the interim. Because rates are always fluctuating, there is a chance the rate could either increase or decrease prior to closing.

Float-down: A type of rate lock, plus the opportunity to lower the rate if market interest rates drop significantly during the loan-processing period. Float-downs are more costly to the borrower because they offer more value and therefore cost the lender more to provide them. Float-downs are diverse in terms of how often (typically once) and when the borrower can exercise this right.

Flood: A temporary overflow of a normally dry area due to overflow of a body of water, unusual buildup, runoff of surface waters, abnormal erosion, or undermining of shoreline. Floods can also be overflow of mudflow caused by a buildup of water underground.

Flood certification: Determination of whether property falls within a designated flood zone.

Flood insurance: This policy protects against losses caused by floods and is required for all properties in specified flood zones.

Flood-prone area: A place with a 1-percent chance of one flood per year and where chances remain that high each year.

Floor plan: Describes how rooms are positioned in a home or other building.

Floor plan insurance: Insurance that covers goods meant for sale in the possession of a retailer and have been accepted as collateral for a loan. If the goods are damaged or destroyed, the lender is covered.

Floor price: The lowest preconceived price a seller will accept.

Flue: The cavity that guides soot and smoke from a fireplace into the chimney.

Following form: A form written in exactly the same terms as other property insurance policies covering a piece of property.

Footing: A grounded concrete support beneath a foundation that bears another structure and distributes its weight evenly. Footings are wider than the things they support.

For sale by owner (FSBO): An owner sells property without using a real estate broker. This owner works directly with the buyer or the buyer's real estate agent.

Forbearance: Granting someone time to fix a problem, such as a loan default, before making any legal moves.

Force majeure: An unstoppable external force that causes parties to breach a contract.

Foreclosure: Someone loses property to settle a mortgage debt they cannot pay. This legal procedure turns the property title over to the mortgage lender or it allows a third party to buy the property, without any encumbrances that would lessen its value, in a foreclosure sale.

Foreign insurer: An insurance company housed in a different state than the one the insured's policy is written in.

Forfeiture: Losing valuable possessions or money by failing to follow a contract.

Form: A document that completes a policy. This term can also mean an endorsement or rider.

Foundation drain tile: A pipe that drains water from a foundation. It can be made of clay.

Foundation exclusion clause: A clause found in fire insurance, stating that the value of a property's foundation will not be calculated in the total property value after a loss.

Foundation walls: Underground walls providing a building's main support. These concrete or masonry walls can also define a basement.

Franchise: Agreement in which a company lets offshoot offices use its name and services for a fee. Franchises in real estate include brokerages working for a national business.

Free and clear title: A property that has no mortgages and no liens. *See also "clear title."*

Free cash flow: Operating income plus amortization and depreciation (noncash charges), but minus charges that use cash, like capital expenditures and dividends. Essentially, the amount of cash left over after doing normal business for a year is free cash flow.

Free-standing building: A structure separate from others, such as a shed by a house.

Front footage: Length, in feet, of the front edge of a piece of land.

Front money: Money someone needs to buy land and prepare it for development.

Front-end fee: Income paid to the mortgage broker from the borrower, as opposed to the back-end fee paid by the lender.

Front-end ratio: A lender's comparison of how much a person pays each month to finance his or her housing and how much money is earned.

Frontage: The foremost part of a lot, which can border a road or body of water.

FSBO: Short for "for sale by owner."

Full doc loan: A mortgage loan that requires proof of all the income, assets, and other financial information of the borrower.

Full disclosure: Keeping nothing secret that could influence a sale. For example, telling the buyer a property's defects.

Full recourse: if the borrower stops repaying the loan, full responsibility goes to its endorser — the person who backed the loan.

Fully amortizing payment: A payment structure in which the payments each month are enough to pay off the principle and interest on a loan by the end of the term. Fixed rate mortgages are generally fully amortizing.

Fully indexed interest rate: Current index value plus margin on an ARM. Initial interest rates are normally below the fully indexed rate, but the rate will rise to full after a period determined by interest rate increase cap, assuming index is unchanged.

Functional obsolescence: A state of lowered value when an improvement is badly designed or loses function, such as a sliding window that sticks and will not open.

Funding fee: Payment for mortgage protections, such as the fee to secure a loan backed by the Department of Veterans Affairs.

Funds from operations (FFO): The net income a REIT generates, not including losses or gains from property sales, and adding real estate depreciation back in. When compared to normal corporate accounting, it is a good approximation of cash flow and considered to be an even better judge of operations than generally accepted accounting principles, the standard for American public companies.

G

Gambrel roof: A roof with two sloping sides. From its top, the slopes descend gently, and then each side takes a steeper angle for its lower part.

Gap in title: A missing link in the history of who has held a title, from when records are incomplete.

Garden apartment: A building in which at least a portion of the tenants can use a common lawn yard.

Garnishment: Resulting from a legal judgment, garnishment means automatic deductions from a borrower's paycheck to repay the lender for outstanding debts.

Gazebo: Small structure found in gardens, backyards, and parks. Gazebos are partially open but roofed.

General (or master) plan: Used by governments to grow communities in an organized way. This long-term program dictates how property will be developed and used.

General contractor: The primary person in charge of a construction project. He or she is contracted to oversee it and can hire subcontractors to handle it.

General real estate tax: Sum of municipality and government taxes on a piece of property.

General warranty deed: The most common and safest deed used when people transfer real estate. The party granting it guarantees sure and clear title to the property.

Generally accepted accounting principles (GAAP): The method by which all publicly traded companies report financial numbers.

Generic prices: Prices that typically display a consistent set of transaction traits, which normally claim the lowest possible prices.

Gift letter: States that money someone will use for a down payment or other purpose came from a friend or relative's gift, creating no debt. People send gift letters to lenders and government agencies.

Gift of equity: Selling a home to a family member or someone else with whom the seller has a close relationship at a price lower than its market value. The gift of equity is the difference between what the house sells for and its actual market value. Most lenders typically let the gift count as the down payment.

Ginnie Mae: *See "Government National Mortgage Association."*

Good fairy syndrome: Having faith there is a "good fairy" somewhere in the world who will get people out of their financial dilemmas.

Good faith estimate (GFE): Total cost of getting a home loan as estimated by a broker or lender, summing all fees the borrower must pay.

Goodwill: The difference between the value at the time of closing shown on the corporate books and the purchase price.

Government loan: A mortgage loan insured or backed by the Department of Veterans Affairs, the Rural Housing Service, or the Federal Housing Administration.

Government National Mortgage Association (GNMA or Ginnie Mae): Like Freddie Mac and Fannie Mae, this federally-owned corporation funds lenders who make home loans. It also buys loans, but only if they are government-backed. These loans are typically given to low income and first time homeowners. Ginnie Mae does not issue or purchase mortgages, but guarantees loans.

Government survey method: A standard way of describing land features used in the majority of U.S. states, especially in the west.

Grace period: A set period of time when someone can make an overdue loan payment before suffering any consequences.

Grade: The height of a hill or slope compared to level ground, including how steeply it angles. To calculate grade, divide the raised area's elevation (in feet) by the number of horizontal feet you would travel to get there on flat ground. If a slope reaches 30 feet high by the time one travels 100 horizontal feet, its grade is 30 percent.

Graduated-payment mortgage (GPM): A mortgage set up with a repayment plan that has payments increasing over a period
of years.

Graduation period: A period of time during which the payment on a GPM goes up.

Graduation rate: The percentage that the payment on a GPM increases.

Grandfather clause: Idea that something built or made under an old set of rules is allowed to stay as it is, even when new rules take over. A building might not comply with new legal codes, but if it was grandfathered in before those rules came, it might be left alone.

Granny flat (in-law apartment): A small space someone rents in a home zoned for a single family.

Grant deed: Grantors of these deeds give recipients their word they have not passed the real estate to anyone else before. They affirm the property has no encumbrances lessening its use or value except what the deed lists. California is known for deals using grant deeds.

Grant: Passage of property to a new owner that people can do using deeds.

Grantee: Usually, the buyer in a real estate transaction.

Grantor: Usually, the seller in a real estate transaction.

Gratuitous agent: Services clients for free.

GRI: Graduate, Realtors® Institute. GRIs are people trained in finance, investing, appraisal, law, and sales as prescribed by the Realtors® Institute.

Gross building area: Summed area of all floors in a building, excluding projecting pieces of architecture or other things not part of the house's bulk. It includes penthouses, basements, and mezzanines part of an outer wall's main surface.

Gross income: The income of a household minus expenses and taxes.

Gross income multiplier: A number used to estimate a property's value. One multiplies the property's yearly gross income by this figure.

Gross leasable area: Total amount of space meant for rent-paying tenants and no one else.

Gross rent multiplier (GRM): A number used in gauging a property's value. One multiplies the property's monthly gross income by this figure.

Ground lease: A lease in which a tenant only rents land, not a building. The tenant may own or construct a building on the land following the lease's rules. Ground leases can last a long time, and they can be net leases, which means the tenant pays the property's maintenance fees and taxes.

Guaranteed Mortgage Price Agreement (GMPA): A presentation for action by HUD in 2002 to let lenders and other financiers provide loan packages and settlement services at one price.

Guaranteed sale program: Brokers can offer this option, agreeing to give a property owner a set amount of money if that person's listed real estate does not sell within a certain time period. The owner is free to buy another house because their previous building is guaranteed to sell.

Guarantor: Someone making a guarantee.

Guaranty: Interaction where someone agrees to settle another's obligations or debt if the other cannot.

Guardian: Person a court selects to manage the property and affairs of a child or someone else who cannot do it alone.

H

Habitable room: Living spaces one counts when summing a home's number of rooms. They exclude corridors and bathrooms.

Handicap: A disability that hinders one's mental or physical functions, limiting at least one life activity described in the Fair Housing Act.

Hard cost: Money spent to build improvements on a property.

Hard-money mortgage: Secured by cash from a borrower rather than real estate. The borrower pays money or pledges the equity of property.

Hazard insurance (homeowner's insurance or fire insurance): Covers property damage by wind, fire, and other destructive forces.

Heirs and assigns: People designated to receive another's property by a deed or will. Assigns receive the interest to a piece of real estate, and heirs inherit a deceased person's property.

Heirs and assigns can will the property they receive to someone else, or they can sell it.

Hiatus: Missing information in a property's ownership history. Also, a hiatus is a gap created between two pieces of land because the legal description is inaccurate.

High rise: A structure exceeding 25 stories tall in a business district or six stories in a suburb.

High-water mark: Property line separating a public waterway and a land parcel. Also, a line showing how far a medium tide comes up a shore.

Highest and best use: Most legal and sensible way one can use property or land to give it peak value in a financially realistic, well-supported way.

Historic structure: A building given special status for tax purposes because it is officially deemed historically important.

Historical scenario: Assuming the index value associated with an adjustable-rate mortgage emulates a similar pattern to that of an index value from earlier years. This practice is typically unhelpful because showing changing mortgage payments on mortgages that were started in the past does not help a borrower. Using that historical information on how it applies to a current mortgage, however, would be helpful.

Hold harmless clause: One party pledging in a contract to guard another against legal actions and claims. Rent contracts may include this term to protect a building owner from lawsuits by a tenant's customers.

Holdback: A chunk of loaned money the lender withholds until a certain event happens, such as builders finishing a house.

Holdback provision: If a buyer has to pay a debt the seller did not disclose, the amount paid is taken from what was held back in an escrow account at closing, as written into the purchase and sell agreement.

Holding company: Owns or manages one or more other companies.

Holding escrow: A situation in which a third party (escrow agent) holds onto a deed's final documents of title.

Holdover tenant: This tenant holds onto a property once the lease ends.

Home equity conversion mortgage (HECM or reverse annuity mortgage): Allows homeowners to turn their home's equity into monthly cash payments, provided by a lender.

Home equity line of credit: A type of second mortgage in which money is taken in draws rather than in one lump sum. Lines of credit are often used to pay for education and home repairs or improvement projects. Money can be borrowed up to the maximum amount of the line of credit.

Home equity loan: A loan someone takes out using his or her house as collateral.

Home improvement loan: A mortgage that finances the renovation of an addition on a home.

Home inspection: A complete, professional inspection of a property intended to check and evaluate the safety of the structure and mechanical condition. An adequate home inspection is often a condition set forth by the purchaser.

Home inspector: A person authorized to assess how operational and structurally sound a property is.

Home keeper: A type of reverse mortgage offered solely by Fannie Mae, in which a homeowner obtains the home's equity and pays it back until he or she does not live in the house anymore.

Home Owners Loan Corporation: A 1933 Congress-established federal government organization put in place to help families avoid foreclosure on their homes.

Home Valuation Code of Conduct (HVCC): This rule was put into effect on May 1, 2009 by Freddie Mac and Fannie Mae. It stated from then on, the agencies would only buy mortgages backed by an independent appraisal.

Homebuyer protection plan: A specific plan intended to safeguard FHA homebuyers against flaws and defects in the property.

Homeowner's insurance policy: A policy for homeowners that provides protection from theft, fire, and other unforeseen losses. *See also "hazard insurance."*

Homeowners' association (HOA): A group enforcing rules or restrictions the developer sets on a neighborhood, condominium, or community. This group collects payments each month for the community's expenses and upkeep.

Homeowners' warranty: Insures devices and systems for heating, cooling, and other purposes over a certain time period, which guarantees they will be fixed if needed.

Homestead deed: A filed declaration in the land records that states someone is asserting his or her homestead exemption. The exemption permits an individual to protect up to $5,000 in assets against creditor claims, plus $500 per dependent.

Homestead exemption: A reduction in the market value of a primary residence for the purpose of calculating property tax. Only available in some states, it gives the homeowner a break on the amount they pay in taxes.

Homestead: Land a family owns and lives on. Parts of this land or its value are safe from legal action relating to debt in certain states.

Hostile possession: *See "adverse possession."*

House rules: They govern the behavior of condominium occupants. Members of the condominium owners' association create these rules to foster peaceful relations between owners and residents.

Housing bank: A housing lender associated with or owned by the government. The U.S. government, with few exceptions, does not loan to customers directly, but several developing countries are home to housing banks.

Housing bubble: A considerable rise in the price of houses produced in part by the belief the prices will keep increasing.

Housing expense: The total sum of property taxes, mortgage payments, homeowner association fees, and hazard insurance.

Housing expense ratio (HER): The portion of gross monthly income someone spends on housing costs, expressed as a percent.

Housing for the elderly: Living space designed to accommodate people 55 or older, with common access areas.

Housing investment: The amount of money a person invests in a house equal to its sale price minus any loan amounts.

Housing starts: The approximate number of construction projects for housing units beginning during a certain time period.

HUD median income: An estimate from the Department of Housing and Urban Development (HUD) of how much money families in a given area earn on average.

HUD-1 Settlement Statement (settlement sheet or closing statement): A detailed list of the funds parties pay when their transaction completes.

Hundred percent location: The spot in a city where land is most valuable, which can mean the rent is highest and vehicle and foot traffic is heaviest.

HVAC: Stands for heating, ventilating, and air conditioning.

Hybrid ARM: A type of adjustable-rate mortgage in which the initial rate remains the same for a certain period of time during which it is deemed a fixed rate. After the period of time ends, it becomes an adjustable rate. This term usually pertains to ARMS with three years or longer of fixed rate periods.

Hybrid REIT: A mixture of the investment strategies of mortgage and equity REITs.

Hypothecate: To back a loan by pledging property but not surrendering it.

I-banker: The abbreviation of investment banker; also known as a merger and acquisition intermediary and, for smaller transactions, known as a business broker.

Illiquidity: Difficulty converting something to cash. Real property is deemed illiquid because turning it into money is not easy.

Impact fee: Private developers pay this fee to the city for permission to start a project. The money helps the city build infrastructure, such as sewers, for the new development.

Implied agency: When a party acts as another party's agent and both show they accept this relationship, they form an implied agency.

Implied equity market cap: The value of all UPREIT partnership units, assuming they are all part of the REIT's stock. This is added to the market value of a company's outstanding common stock. This measurement does not include warrants, convertible preferred stock, and convertible debentures.

Implied listing: An agreement in which parties show their concurrence by how they act.

Implied warranty of habitability: In this legal theory, landlords imply property for rent is fit to live on and to use for its intended purpose.

Impound: Portion of a mortgage payment set apart and saved to cover private mortgage insurance, pay real estate taxes, and insure property against hazards.

Improved land: Land with some development or construction, whether people can live there or not.

Improvement: Any construction that boosts a property's value, including private structures such as buildings and fences, as well as public structures such as roads and water piping.

Improvements: Changes that make a building or property more valuable, useful, or enjoyable.

In-house sale: A kind of sale made solely by the broker in the listing agreement, with no other brokers involved. This kind of sale includes situations in which the broker finds the buyer or the buyer approaches someone working for the broker.

Income approach: A way to estimate how much a moneymaking property is worth. One predicts how much net income the property will make each year through its entire life and capitalizes that income, which determines its present value.

Income property: A piece of real estate used by the owner to earn money without residing there.

Income statement: A document reporting someone's financial history, including the amounts of money made and expenses paid, where that money came from and went, and how much the subject profited or lost. It can report on cash or accruals.

Incorporation by reference: Adding terms to a given document by referencing the other documents where they appear.

Incurable obsolescence: A flaw on a property that cannot be fixed or is too expensive to merit repairs.

Indemnify: Guard another against harm or loss.

Indenture: An agreement on paper between at least two people whose interests differ. An indenture can also be a deed with reciprocal commitments the parties agree to fulfill.

Independent contractor: Someone hired to achieve a result through means they choose and control. Independent contractors get no employee benefits, and they must pay their own expenses and taxes. Real estate brokers are known to operate this way.

Index: A table of financial information that lenders use to determine how much interest a borrower will pay on an adjustable-rate mortgage.

Index loan: A long-lasting loan for which payment amounts change in tune with a certain index.

Indexed ARM: An adjustable rate mortgage in which the interest rate, based on an interest rate index, is automatically adjusted.

Indicated value: How much a piece of real estate is worth, depending on its land value and its cost minus depreciation; the net income it makes during yearly operations; and how much similar properties currently sell for.

Indirect costs: Money spent on development for things besides the labor and materials going directly into structures on the lot.

Indoor air quality: Degree of pollution in a building from smoke, radon, or other gaseous contaminants.

Industrial park: A zone meant for manufacturing and for related projects and entities.

Informed consent: Choosing to permit something after learning enough details to inform one's decision.

Infrastructure: Utility lines, roads, sewers, and other public developments meant to meet people's basic needs in a subdivision or city.

Ingress and Egress: When applied to easements, the right to enter and leave a property but not the right to park on the property.

Initial interest rate: The starting interest rate for an adjustable-rate mortgage. It can fluctuate over time and change the borrower's monthly mortgage payments.

Initial public offering (IPO): A company's first sale of stock to the public.

Initial rate duration: How long an adjustable-rate mortgage is set to keep the interest rate it started with.

Injunction: When a court compels someone to do or not do a certain act.

Innocent misrepresentation: When someone lies accidentally.

Innocent purchaser: A party who buys contaminated property without knowing it is tainted despite having it investigated beforehand. This buyer bears no obligation to clean it up.

Inquiry notice: The notice that laws suppose a reasonable individual would gain if he inquired into a property.

Inside lot: Surrounded on three sides by other lots and fronted by a road, unlike a corner lot with two sides bordering roads.

Inspection: Done prior to the purchase of a home to ensure the house is in good condition without major damage or structural flaws. In some cases, the lender will require an inspection for financing. This is always required for FHA loans. The buyer has the right to hire a private inspector prior to purchasing the property. In most cases, the agreement of sale is contingent upon passing the inspection.

Inspection report: A document prepared by a licensed inspector that describes the condition of a property.

Installment contract (contract for deed or articles of agreement for warranty deed): Lets a buyer make gradual payments for real estate. Meanwhile, the buyer possesses the property, but its title remains with the seller for a time, possibly until the buyer finishes paying.

Installment note: Calls for the buyer to pay for the property in specific amounts over time.

Institutional lenders: Entities that invest in loans and other securities as a business, by using others' funds they manage or their own money. The law regulates the loans institutional lenders make.

Instrument: A legal statement in writing establishing parties' rights, relationship, or required duties, such as a contract.

Insulation disclosure: Open sharing of details about the insulation in a house required of real estate brokers and anyone building or selling new homes. They disclose the insulation's thickness, components, and effectiveness (R-value).

Insurable title: Can get coverage from title insurance companies.

Insurance binder: Provides coverage temporarily until one can set up a permanent policy.

Insured mortgage: Guaranteed through private mortgage insurance or the Federal Housing Administration.

Intangibles: Nonphysical assets, such as licenses, trademarks, franchises, customer lists, unpatented technology, etc.

Interest: A fee borrowers pay lenders alongside loan repayments. Lenders charge debtors interest for using their loaned money.

Interest accrual period: The time when interest due to lender is determined. For example, for a 4-percent mortgage on $200,000 during a monthly period, the interest would be $.04/12(\$200,000)$ = \$666.67.

Interest cost: The cost, adjusted by time, to a mortgage borrower.

Interest due: The interest amount, determined by multiplying the loan balance at the end of the last term by the annual interest rate divided by the accrual period.

Interest in property: A share owned in a property by law.

Interest payment: The interest paid every month, expressed in a dollar amount. The interest payment is the same as the interest due as long as the interest due is less than or equal to the scheduled mortgage payment. If this is not the case, the interest payment is the same as the scheduled payment.

Interest rate: Money charged to the loan amount as the fee for the money's use.

Interest rate adjustment period: After the initial rate period, this is how frequently the adjustable-rate mortgage rates adjust. For example, with a 2/2 ARM, both periods are two years, but a 2/1 ARM has an initial period of two years, with rates adjusting every year after that.

Interest rate cap: This is a provision in adjustable-rate mortgages that limits how much an interest rate can increase. There are periodic interest rate caps, which limit increases during each adjustment period. Most loans also have lifetime caps, a limit that dictates how many percentage points the interest rate can grow over the loan's life.

Interest rate ceiling: The highest possible interest rate in an ARM contract, same as a lifetime cap. The interest rate ceiling is sometimes shown as a certain number of percentage points greater than the initial interest rate.

Interest rate floor: The lowest possible interest rate in an ARM contract. These rates are not as regularly occurring as ceiling rates.

Interest rate index: The series to which an ARM interest rate belongs to, such as "Treasury Funds." These are published in available sources regularly.

Interest rate risk premium: The premium attached to the interest rate above the rate on the loan that poses the smallest risk.

Interest-only loan: In this type of mortgage, the borrower pays the monthly interest on a loan and makes no payments against the debt itself.

Interest-rate buy-down plans: *See "buy-down."*

Interim financing: *See "bridge loan."*

Intermediary: An agent expected to facilitate transactions and who is a merger and acquisition consultant to the buyer or seller.

Internal rate of return (IRR): This measurement allows an investor to calculate a total return, incorporating the return on investment and the return of an investment into the equation. It is used to determine the percentage rate of return of all future cash receipts balanced against all cash contributions, so when each receipt and cash contribution is discounted to net present value, the sum is equal to zero when added together. This is a popular way of measuring a total return on an investment.

Internet mortgages: Mortgages transferred via the Internet, which holds a large role in the process of communication between the lender and the person borrowing.

Interstate Land Sales Full Disclosure Act: A nationwide law governing how real estate transactions between states will work.

Interval ownership: *See "time-share ownership plan."*

Intestate: If the owner of a property dies without a functioning will. Then the state laws of descent determine who inherits the property.

Intrinsic value: The worth a piece of real estate has because it is a kind of property the buyer happens to favor.

Investment bank: A firm that helps make new companies public by underwriting their offerings.

Investment banker: An agent who sometimes provides extra services, such as bridge loans or underwritings.

Investment clubs: Clubs that concentrate on how to grow and invest money wisely.

Investment property: Real estate used to earn money.

Investment structure: Strategic doling out of investment money to different entities that will manage it via loans, joint ventures, leveraged acquisitions, participating debt, triple-net leases, and convertible debt.

Involuntary conversion: When a property's status or ownership changes without the current owner's consent. A house destroyed by a flood or condemned is involuntarily converted.

Involuntary lien: A lien against a property made without the owner's consent. For instance, governments can lay involuntary liens on properties if owners fail to pay taxes.

Ironclad agreement: Unbreakable by anyone taking part.

Irrevocable consent: Approval a party gives that it cannot take back or cancel.

Issuer: A company selling its stock or other securities.

J

Joint liability and joint several liability: Owners each bear total liability for all damages.

Joint note: When two or more makers share equal accountability in a note.

Joint tenancy (tenancy in common): People equally sharing ownership of a property. If one of them dies, the others receive his or her share.

Joint venture: Two or more people joined together as a single business entity to conduct their business for pure profit. This type of venture differs from a partnership in that its business acts as a single venture instead of a continuing business, but a joint venture is legally treated almost like a partnership.

Judgment: A conclusion reached by a court. If the judgment deals with repaying a debt, a lien may be placed by the court against the debtor's real estate as collateral for the individual's creditor.

Judgment lien: Claim laid via legal judgment against property owned by someone in debt.

Judicial foreclosure: A civil lawsuit turning over real estate to a lender or third party because the property owner fails to pay debts. Using civil lawsuits for foreclosure is standard in certain states.

Jumbo loan: A massive mortgage that Freddie Mac and Fannie Mae cannot take on.

Junior lien: A second mortgage or other obligation that will not be the first claim a property owner addresses. The owner must satisfy a more important lien before addressing the junior lien.

Junk fees: An unfavorable term used to describe lender fees, given in dollars as opposed to a percentage of the loan total.

Just compensation: Fair price the government pays a property owner when using eminent domain to render the land public.

K

Key lot: Property desired for its location, which can allow the owner to use adjacent lots to their full potential. Also, a key lot is a property with its front on a secondary street and one side bordering the rear of a corner lot.

Key tenant: An important renter who leases copious space in a shopping center or other complex.

Kicker: Additional fee a debtor pays beyond a mortgage's interest and principal.

Kitchenette: Measuring less than 60 square feet, this area is for handling and cooking food.

Knockdown: Unassembled, premade building materials sent to a construction site for assembly and installation.

L

Land banker: Entity that develops land for future construction and inventories improved pieces of land for later uses.

Land description: Legal account of what a piece of property is like.

Land grant: Land the government provides for colleges specializing in agriculture or for other developments, such as roads and railroads.

Land leaseback: Deal in which an owner sells land and becomes a renting tenant leasing from the new owner. This lease covers the land but not construction upon it. When the lease ends, any structures built on the property go back to the party who originally owned it.

Land trust: A trust a landowner creates that recognizes only one asset: real estate.

Land use map: A map displaying different uses of land in a certain area, along with how much is used and to what degree.

Landlocked: A property bounded by other lots, not directly bordering a road.

Landlord: A person who leases property to someone else.

Landlord's warrant: Legal permission for a landlord to take a tenant's property and publicly sell it to drive the tenant to pay late rent or other fees.

Late charge: Additional money a lender demands when the debtor misses due payments.

Late payment: Money a borrower pays a lender after it was due.

Latent defect: A structural flaw an inspection misses that can pose a hazard to residents. Certain states require licensees and sellers to check for latent defects and reveal any they find.

Leaching cesspool: A cesspool that leaks contents into the soil.

Lead generation: When technology is used to generate new leads for the mortgage broker. This can be done through the use of a database or a computer program. Online lead generation services promise a large number of leads for a price. Some of these companies offer a good service, but others only sell lists of names and tend to sell these lists to more than one broker. Do some research if using a lead generation company to be sure you are getting what you are paying for.

Lead poisoning: Dangerous illness from lead building up in body tissues.

Leads: Prospective clients in the market for a home loan and interested in working with a mortgage broker. There are a variety of ways to get leads. Once the mortgage broker receives a lead about a prospective client, he needs to contact the client and sell his or her brokerage services. Mortgage brokers are continually cultivating leads to generate new business.

Lease: A verbal or written agreement that a tenant will pay for exclusive access to a landlord's property over a certain time period. State laws require long-term leases to be written out, such as agreements exceeding one year.

Lease option/purchase: Allows a person to rent a home and apply part of their lease payments toward purchasing it later.

Leasehold estate: The mortgagor's right of possession of the leased property as outlined in a long-term lease. The agreement between the tenant and landlord spells out the respective obligations of each party.

Leasehold improvements: Fixtures a tenant installs or buys for a property. The tenant can legally remove them when the lease ends if doing so leaves no damage.

Leasehold state: Situation in which someone holds a real estate title by leasing the property long term, not owning it.

Legal age: How old people must be to bear legal responsibility for their actions. One must be 18 to enter real estate agreements or contracts.

Legal description: An account of what a certain parcel looks like, detailed enough that an independent surveyor could find and recognize it.

Legal notice: Giving legal notice means making others aware of something in whatever fashion the law requires. A tenant gives a landlord written legal notice before ending a lease.

Legatee: Someone given property through a will.

Lender: Generally, the same as a broker; someone who loans money.

Lender policy: A title insurance policy that covers the lender against loss related to liens or other encumbrances on the title to a property.

Lender's title insurance: A title insurance policy that covers the lender for the entire amount of the loan. The coverage declines as the loan is paid down, and there is no further coverage once the loan is paid off.

Lessee: Someone renting property through a lease.

Lessor: Someone leasing property to another person.

Let: To lease real estate to a tenant, unlike subletting, which involves the tenant renting the property to someone else.

Letter of intent: An initial, typically nonbinding offer to purchase a business. If the seller accepts the letter of intent, it leads to the drafting of a purchase and sell agreement.

Leverage: The amount of debt in comparison to equity capital or total capital. In real estate, more leverage means a greater risk and a greater potential payoff. If an investment carries a high margin or leverage, it holds that it will carry higher risk, as even a small decline in the asset's value will wreak havoc on the entire investment.

Leverage buyout: When a company's capital stock or assets are purchased in a transaction with borrowed money; it causes the new capital structure of the company to be mainly in debt.

Levy: To set the tax rate on a piece of property after assessing it. To levy is also to collect or take. Seizing property to settle a debt is called levying an execution.

Liabilities: Debts to repay or obligations to fulfill.

Liability insurance: Guards owners against claims of property damage, negligence, or personal injury.

LIBOR (London Interbank Offered Rate): One kind of index lenders use to set and change interest rates on adjustable-rate mortgages, known for its use with interest-only mortgages.

License: The right to broker real estate, given by a state. A license can also mean any right a person holds and cannot sell, or permission, which can be withdrawn, to use land for a time.

Lien: A claim laid on property that can encourage the owner to settle a debt or obligation. Liens allow lenders to sell property if owners do not repay their debts.

Lien statement (offset statement): Statement describing how much debt remains to be paid against a lien on real estate, its due date, interest to be paid, and claims declared.

Lien waiver: Document contractors sign giving up the right to make claims on a property once they have been paid for their work.

Life-care facility: A home for senior citizens that gives medical care.

Life cap: A set restriction on how much an interest rate for an adjustable-rate mortgage can increase or decrease over the mortgage's lifetime.

Light industry: Zoning name for manufacturing companies that are not loud, polluting, or otherwise disruptive.

Limitations of actions: Window of time to take a legal action before it becomes prohibited.

Limited liability company: Joint ownership in which individuals are protected because they do not bear full liability. The participants are considered partners for tax purposes.

Limited partnership: A type of partnership in which one or more general partners manage the business together, which causes all to be responsible for its debts. This special partnership also includes one or more limited partners, some of whom take no part in its management and are therefore not responsible for any debts.

Limited referral agent: A licensed real estate salesperson who refers sellers and buyers to brokerages and gets paid when a deal closes.

Limited warranty deed: Warranties that only cover the time period the last person held a title before passing it on — not time with its previous owners. Any problems that arose when those earlier owners had the property do not fall under warranty.

Line of credit: Credit a financial institution grants a borrower for a specific time period, with a set maximum limit.

Line of sight easement: A right stating one cannot block the view on an easement's land.

Line stakes: Stakes marking the edge of a piece of land.

Lineal foot: A horizontal line across the ground measuring one foot long.

Liquid asset: Any asset easily exchanged for money.

Liquidity: The conversion of assets into cash with no significant loss in value. A higher liquidity signifies it will be an easy conversion, while a lower liquidity signifies it will be a more difficult transition.

Listing agreement: A relationship in which the owner of real estate pays or otherwise compensates a broker to lease or sell property under certain conditions and for a specific price.

Listing broker: The person whose office makes the listing agreement who can also work directly with the buyer.

Listing: Indicates a formal agreement has been signed giving the real estate agent permission to sell the property the listing covers.

Loan application fee: Fee borrowers pay lenders to review their applications for loans.

Loan: Money made available to an individual with set terms for repayment, usually with an interest rate attached.

Loan amount: The amount specified in the mortgage contract that the borrower agrees to pay back. The amount of points included and various other costs make the loan amount different from the quantity of cash distributed by the lender.

Loan churning: The method of occasionally raising money through consecutive cash-out refinances. Loan churning is a hoax started by mortgages brokers to deceive wholesale lenders and dupe unsuspecting borrowers.

Loan discount fee: A fee paid to the lender at the beginning of the lending process for a lower interest rate.

Loan officer: Someone who officially represents a lending institution, with limited power to act for it.

Loan origination fee: The fee the lender charges when a borrower takes out a loan. *See also "origination fee."*

Loan parameters: The factors used to determine whether or not to provide a loan to the borrower.

Loan processor: A loan processor completes several tasks on behalf of the lender. Mortgage brokers sometimes employ loan processors to handle some of the paperwork on behalf of the broker. The processor takes the application, checks the credit, arranges for appraisals, and generally assists the broker or lender in the process.

Loan servicing: The steps lending institutions take with each loan. They include managing borrowers' payments and issuing statements; collecting on loans past due; making sure owners pay their taxes and insurance on a property; handling escrow/impound accounts; and further tasks, such as managing assumptions and payoffs.

Loan-to-value ratio (LTV ratio): Comparison between the sum loaned as a mortgage and the value of the collateral property securing the loan.

Location, location, location: An expression stressing how much a property's location influences its value.

Lock: The process that allows a borrower to lock the interest rate on a loan. Once the rate is locked, it will not change if interest rates increase or decrease while the borrower is waiting to go to closing.

Lock box: A locked metal box attached to the door of a for-sale property that holds the key to property. Only agents holding the code or key can open the box.

Lock commitment letter: A lender's written acknowledgement that a loan's price and certain other terms have been locked. Borrowers using mortgage brokers to lock their loans should play it safe and require the broker to show the commitment letter.

Lock failure: When a lender is incapable or unwilling to honor a mortgage price presumed by the borrower to be unquestionably guaranteed.

Lock jumper: A borrower who lets a lock run out when interest rates lower so as to lock in again at an even lower rate. These borrowers are typically refinancing a home rather than buying one.

Lock-in: A lender's promise to charge a borrower a certain interest rate for a specific time span.

Lock-in period: The time span for which a lender promises a borrower a certain interest rate.

Loft: Unfinished building space. Also, open area on the two lowest floors that accommodates retail or manufacturing.

Long-term lease: Rental contract lasting three or more years before ending or being renewed.

Lot and block (recorded plat) system: A way to identify plots of land in a subdivision, using numbers for lots and blocks as they appear on a map called a subdivision plat.

Low rise: A structure standing four stories or fewer above ground.

Low-documentation loan: A mortgage for which borrowers provide only fundamental proof of their assets and income.

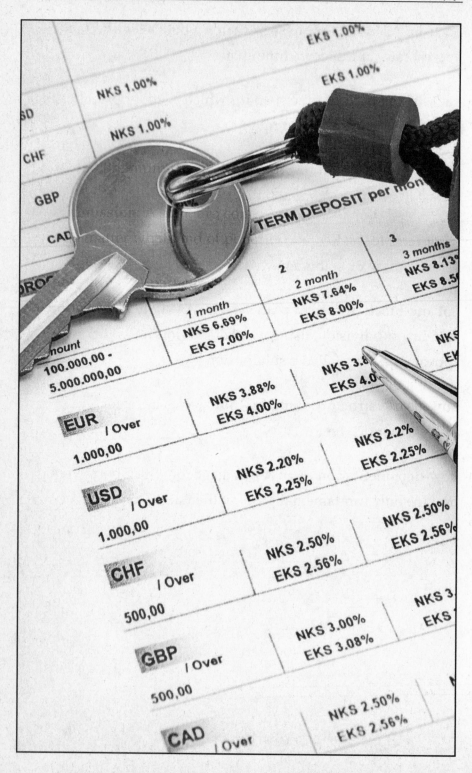

M

M & A: The acronym for mergers and acquisitions.

Maggie Mae (Mortgage Guarantee Insurance Corporation, MGIC): Provides insurance for those investing in mortgage loans.

Maintenance fee: Monthly fee paid by people in homeowner's associations to maintain and mend common parts of the property they live in.

Mandatory disclosure: Various mortgage regulations and laws that set up the rules on which information must be revealed to borrowers, as well as when and how the information must be disclosed.

Manufactured housing: Houses completely built inside a factory and then moved to and installed on the site of choice. These houses are typically built without prior knowledge of where they will be transported and are liable to be subjected to federal building codes authorized by HUD.

Maps and plats: Surveys showing the features of land parcels, including area measures, landmarks, property lines, who owns them, and more.

Margin: A number added to the index determining interest rates on adjustable-rate mortgage. It adjusts the numbers in the index to create the interest rate a borrower gets. A margin can also be a percentage tacked onto that index through the term of the mortgage.

Market cap: Abbreviation for market capitalization that applies to the company's worth in the stock market by multiplying the total number of outstanding shares by the current price of the stock.

Market conditions: Marketplace traits such as demographics and rates of interest, employment, vacancies, property sales, and leases.

Market data approach (sales comparison approach): Gauging a property's value by comparing it with similar real estate sold recently.

Market rents: The same as a CMA, only on rental units; the market rents are rents gained in comparison to other rentals in the same location.

Market study: Estimation of future demand for particular real estate projects, including possible rental fees and square feet sold or leased.

Market value: The going price a property could sell for at any given point in time. For mortgaging purposes, the mortgage lender typically uses the property's appraised value to determine market value.

Marketable title: Legitimate, clearly held title at low risk of lawsuits for flaws.

Master deed: Used by condominium developers to record development on the whole property, broken down into units people own.

Master lease: The main lease controlling all following leases. It may encompass more real estate than the entire group of subsequent leases.

Maturity date: The day by which a borrower must fully repay a loan.

Maturity: The date a loan becomes due or a contract ends.

Maximum loan amount: The most money permitted to be loaned out in a specific loan program. Some loan maximums are decided by individual lenders. When programs target the loan to be for sale to Freddy Mac or Fannie Mae, the maximum is considered the biggest loan available for the agencies to buy. FHA loan maximums are decided by the Federal Housing Administration and can differ based on geographic location.

Maximum loan-to-value ratio: The highest loan-to-value ratio allowed within the chosen loan program.

Maximum lock: The most extensive period of time for which the lender can lock the points and rate in a particular program. Sixty days is the most frequently used maximum lock term, though some programs go up to 90 days as the maximum lock; few programs exceed a period of 90 days.

Mechanic's lien: Used by contractors and others involved in building on property to ensure they get paid. This claim lasts until the workers are compensated for services and supplies rendered for construction, improvement, or repair.

Merged credit report: Combines data from Experian, Equifax, and TransUnion—three major credit bureaus.

Merger: The uniting of at least two investments, companies, or other interests.

Mesne: Intermediate; represents the middle ground between two extreme positions, especially rank or time.

Metes and bounds: A survey system that does not use lot numbers. Instead, this system uses natural features of the land, such as rivers and trees, as well as neighboring landowners, along with specific distances to describe plots of land.

Metropolitan statistical area (MSA): One or more counties with a population of at least 50,000.

Mezzanine: A floor midway between a structure's major stories or between the ceiling and floor in a single-story building.

Mezzanine financing: A blend of equity and debt that takes second priority behind a primary loan. It allows lenders to possess property if the borrower does not pay the debt.

Micropolitan statistical area: An urban cluster with a population ranging from 10,000 to 49,000 people.

Middle market: Companies that sell between $2 million and $100 million.

Mid-rise: A structure four to eight stories tall or as high as 25 stories in business districts.

Mile: 5,280 feet (1,760 yards).

Minimum down payment: In any program, the minimum down payment is the smallest permissible correlation of the down payment in relation to the sale price. For example, if the minimum is 10 percent, the down payment on a house costing $100,000 must be at least $10,000.

Minimum lot area: Lowest lot size a subdivision permits. Such small lots would not suit acreage zoning, which calls for spacious properties.

Minimum property requirements: Conditions property must meet before the Federal Housing Administration will underwrite a mortgage. The home must be reliably built, habitable, and up to housing standards in its location.

Miniperm loan: This is used as a temporary loan between a construction loan and a permanent loan.

Mixed use: A multipurpose part of a property, such as space for business and residency.

Mobile home: A manufactured home delivered somewhere, able to relocate.

Model home: A home exemplifying others being developed. Model homes are furnished and displayed for buyers as part of an effort to sell other homes in a development.

Modification: Changes made to the terms of a mortgage without refinancing.

Modular housing: Housing manufactured off-site and delivered to a site in pieces.

Month-to-month tenancy: Someone paying rent month-by-month, with no longer commitment. This is the default situation if the landlord and tenant make no rental agreement. Month-to-month tenancy can take over after a lease expires.

Monthly debt service: The required payments made every month on credit cards, home equity loans, installment loans, and other debt commitments. It does not include payments on the loan that was applied for.

Monument: A natural or manmade landmark used to create property lines for a surveyor's description of real estate.

Moratorium: Time period during which payments are not required or certain acts are prohibited.

Mortgage: Borrowed money for buying real estate, with the purchased property for collateral.

Mortgage-backed securities: These are securities sold on the stock market backed by the principal and interest payments on a pool of mortgage loans. A large number of mortgages are bundled together and sold as mortgage-backed securities. This generates more money for future mortgaging lending. These are residential mortgage loans. There are also commercial mortgage-backed securities, which are secured by commercial or multifamily properties.

Mortgage banker: An institution that uses its own funds to make home loans, which mortgage investors and insurance companies can buy.

Mortgage broker: Someone who pairs loan-seekers with mortgage lenders. Brokers are approved to work with certain lenders.

Mortgage calculator: A tool or program used to determine a mortgage's monthly payments. These calculators use the amount financed, term of the loan, and interest rate to calculate the monthly payment.

Mortgage company: A type of moneylender that sells all mortgage loans in the secondary market. The companies might service the loans they create, or they might not.

Mortgage formulas: Equations used to determine a mortgage market's regular methods, such as balances, monthly payments, and APR.

Mortgage grader: A mortgage broker website that has several appealing components, as well as some not as attractive features.

Mortgage insurance (MI): Protects lenders from particular consequences if borrowers fail to repay loans. Lenders can require mortgage insurance for certain loans.

Mortgage insurance premium (MIP): The price of mortgage insurance, paid to private companies or governments.

Mortgage interest deduction: A tax deduction homeowners get for paying yearly interest on mortgages.

Mortgage lead: A loan provider's collection of information on consumers that have the potential to be converted into borrowers. People become leads when they complete online questionnaires about themselves in response to certain ads.

Mortgage lender: A company that lends money to borrowers for the purchase of homes.

Mortgage life and disability insurance: A type of life insurance that covers the borrower in the event of death, automatically satisfying the debt. The borrower may also be covered for disability, allowing for the insurance to make payments while the borrower is disabled. Depending on the terms of coverage, the policy may not start until after a specific period following the disability.

Mortgage modification: An alteration in the loan terms, typically in the term itself or in the interest rate, as an acknowledgement that the borrower cannot make the payments as outlined in the current contract.

Mortgage note: A written debt agreement secured by a mortgage that includes the repayment details, such as the debt amount and how the debt must be repaid.

Mortgage payment: The payment made each month by the borrower that includes both interest and principal.

Mortgage preapproval: When a lender determines that a borrower has the finances and credit to merit a particular loan with specified terms.

Mortgage program: A group of characteristics attributed to a type of mortgage, including type, term, initial rate period, and if it is insured.

Mortgage price: The sum of the points, interest rate, and all fees paid to the mortgage broker and/or lender. The maximum rate and the fully indexed rate are included in the mortgage price of an ARM.

Mortgage referrals: Recommendations from acquaintances on where to obtain a mortgage.

Mortgage REIT: A REIT that makes or owns loans and other obligations obtained by real estate collateral. This term also refers to REITs that lend money in nonmortgage transactions, such as mezzanine or a bridge loan.

Mortgage scams: Plots concocted by brokers, lenders, home sellers, and occasionally even borrowers that are dishonest and deceitful.

Mortgage shopping: Attempting to get the greatest bargain on a mortgage.

Mortgage spam: Offers that spontaneously show up in your e-mail about terrific mortgage deals.

Mortgage suitability: The widely held belief that, when mortgage lenders supply unsuitable loans to a borrower, the lender should be held responsible.

Mortgage term: The amount of time in which the borrower must repay the mortgage loan. This is generally 15 or 30 years, depending on the loan.

Mortgagee: The mortgage lender.

Mortgagor: One who borrows money from a mortgage lender.

Mud room: A small chamber opening to a play place or yard. Mudrooms can house laundry machines.

Mudsill: A building's lowest horizontal part — possibly laid in or on the ground.

Multidwelling units: Collected properties housing more than one family but covered by one mortgage.

Multiple listing clause: A clause requiring and authorizing a broker to share a listing he or she manages with other brokers.

Multiple Listing Service (MLS): A group of brokers who share listing agreements and hope to find suitable buyers quickly. Acceptable listings include exclusive-agency and exclusive-right-to-sell types.

Multiple listing: Sharing of information and profit between real estate brokers. They agree to give one another details about listings and to split commissions from the sales.

Municipal ordinances: Laws by local governments regarding standards for subdivisions and buildings.

Narrative report: An appraisal written in explanatory paragraphs, not a letter, table, or form.

National Association of Realtors®: A group of real estate agents working toward best practice in their field.

National Housing Act of 1968: An act that formed programs to promote the building of low-income housing.

Negative amortization: Happens when a borrower makes monthly payments smaller than the adjustable-rate mortgage's interest rate. The leftover interest builds up and adds to the unpaid balance.

Negative amortization cap: This is the limit of negative amortization allowed on an adjustable-rate mortgage. The cap is expressed as a percentage of the total amount of the loan.

Negative cash flow: Occurs when a property makes too little income to pay for its own operations.

Negative homeowner's equity: When a person owes more on the home than it is actually worth.

Negative points: Paid by a lender for a rate above that of a zero-point load, usually referred to as "rebates" or, in the case of a mortgage broker, "yield spread premium." For example, the following: 8 percent/0 points, 7 percent/3 points, 9 percent/-3 points.

Net after taxes: Income a property makes minus its operating costs and taxes.

Net asset value (NAV): The commonly accepted market value of a company's assets and properties after taking out its obligations and liabilities. This measurement tool, though popular for many REIT investors, is not fully comprehensive because it only relies on property assets.

Net branch: A facility offered to mortgage brokers by a lender that causes the brokers to become employees of the lender while also maintaining independent status. An advantage is brokers do not have to disclose yield spread premiums given by lenders.

Net income: The profits a business earns after expenses are subtracted from revenues. Real estate depreciation is considered an expense under Generally Accepted Accounting Principles (GAAP).

Net jumping: Using the Internet to secure a loan after already having used a broker's expert knowledge and time to become creditworthy and well versed in matters concerning loans.

Net lease: It calls for a tenant to pay taxes, insurance, utilities, and upkeep expenses for a property, along with rent.

Net operating income (NOI): A property's income before taxes, with expected vacancies and operating costs factored in.

Net present value: The difference between an investment's present value of expected cash flow and the invested amount.

Net sales proceeds: Money made by selling part or all of an asset, minus costs from closing the sale, paying a broker, and marketing the property.

Net usable acres: Part of a plot appropriate for construction, minus land that cannot be built on because of building code restrictions, such as zoning or density rules.

Net worth: A company's value, determined using the worth of its total assets minus all liabilities.

Networking: Maintaining contacts with a variety of people connected with buying and selling businesses.

Niche market: A term used to describe a specialized segment of a particular market. For example, in the mortgage brokerage business, a niche market would be a specific group of potential borrowers with which a broker specializes. Examples of niche markets include police officers, teachers, and self-employed individuals.

No asset loan: A documentation specification in which the assets of the applicant are not revealed.

No cash out refinance (rate-and-term refinance): Refinancing of a mortgage designed to cover only its remaining debt and fees for getting a second loan.

No change scenario: Believing that, on an ARM, the financial worth of the index to which the rate is connected does not shift from its beginning value.

No deal/no commission clause: A contract clause stating a broker gets paid only if the property title changes hands as the contract specifies.

No Fee Mortgage Plus: A program for homebuyers through Bank of America that removes all lender fees except points, as well as removes all third-party fees.

No income loan: A documentation specification where the income of the applicant is not revealed.

No ratio loan: A documentation specification in which the income of the borrower is revealed and confirmed but is not used in the process of qualifying the applicant. Income and expense, the common maximum ratios, are not used in this situation.

No-cost loan: Has a higher interest rate but no associated fees.

No-documentation loan: Given for a large down payment to people with good credit. Applicants need not verify their assets or income.

No-surprise adjustable-rate mortgage: An ARM with a predetermined and graduated payment, as well as in conjunction with variable term.

Nominal interest rate: An interest rate that has been quoted and is neither altered for inflation nor for intra-year compounding. For example, a 5 percent quoted rate on a mortgage is nominal.

Nominee: Someone who represents another, within limits. This can include buying real estate for someone else.

Noncompete clause: Part of a lease stating only a certain tenant's company can do business on a property.

Nonconforming loan: A loan too large or otherwise unsuitable for Freddie Mac or Fannie Mae to buy.

Nonconforming use: A way of utilizing property prohibited by zoning laws but allowed because it began before those ordinances existed.

Nondisclosure: Keeping a fact hidden, whether purposefully or accidentally.

Nondisclosure agreement (NDA): A document signed by two or more negotiating parties, who agree not to share information about one another with those outside of the negotiations.

Noninstitutional lender: A lender that is not part of an institution, such as private individuals, retirement funds, and endowed universities.

Nonjudicial foreclosure: Selling property because its owner fails to pay the mortgage but not working through a court of law. This form of foreclosure might deter title insurers from providing a policy later.

Nonrecourse loan: Does not hold the borrower personally responsible if he or she fails to pay.

Nonpermanent resident alien: A noncitizen who holds employment in the United States but does not have a green card. Nonpermanent resident aliens are more liable to be subjected to selective specifications for qualification than citizens of the United States.

Nonwarrantable condo: A condominium that falls short of adhering to specific requirements set by the lender.

Normal wear and tear: Normal degradation of property with time and usage. It involves things such as small scratches on countertops or tramping down of carpet.

Notary public: Someone legally approved to witness and certify that deeds, mortgages, and other contracts or agreements are carried out. A notary public can also give oaths, take affidavits, and perform other duties.

Note: A written debt instrument a borrower signs to acknowledge the debt and their responsibility to repay the debt.

Notice of default: A document sent to notify people they have defaulted on their loans and are open to legal action.

Notice to quit: Tells a tenant to leave rented property by a certain date or to remedy a problem, such as overdue rent. This document is also called an eviction notice.

Nuisance: Actions on a property that keep others from using nearby land to the fullest. Examples include making loud noises, letting pets wander, or producing pollutants in subdivisions that do not allow these things.

O

Observed condition: A way to appraise how much value a property has lost by assessing how much it has degraded, lost function, or grown obsolete relative to surrounding areas.

Obsolescence: Lessened value in property because it is outdated because its components function less well or it cannot compare with surrounding property.

Occupancy agreement: Allows the buyer to use a piece of real estate before the escrow closes. The buyer gives the seller money for rent.

Occupancy permit: A permit signifying a property meets safety and health standards necessary for it to be habitable. Local governments issue occupancy permits.

Occupancy rate: Percent of space in a building currently being rented.

OEM: The acronym for "original equipment manufacturers." These produce products that are sold to other companies that in turn make products for consumer purchases.

Off-balance sheet items: Obligations left unrecorded, such as unfunded pensions, repurchase agreements, and pending lawsuits.

Off-site management: Administration of property from a distance.

Off-street parking: Found on private land.

Offer and acceptance: Needed for a successful real estate sale contract.

Offer: Stated wish to sell real estate or buy it at a certain cost. Also, a selling price for securities or loans.

Offer to lease: Document meant to lead to an official lease. This offer is made to help the owner and renter agree on lease terms.

Office exclusive: A listing handled by one real estate office only or kept from a Multiple Listing Service by the seller.

Offset statement: *See "lien statement."*

On or before: An expression meaning something is due by a specific date.

On-site management: Duties a property manager must perform while present at the property.

One hundred percent commission: An agreement between salesperson and broker in which the salesperson pays the broker administrative fees and then keeps all the commission from certain sales.

Open listing: In this contract, the seller pays a broker only if the broker finds a suitable buyer before the seller or another broker does.

Open space: Area of water or land devoted to people's enjoyment or use, whether private or public.

Open-end loan: Can increase to a certain amount, keeping the original mortgage as its backing.

Operating budget: A financial plan for moneymaking property based on logically predicted spending and income.

Operating expense: Normal expenses of running operations on a piece of real estate.

Opinion of title: A certificate giving an attorney's opinion of whether someone has valid title to the property for sale.

Option: A legal agreement that gives exclusive right for a person to buy real estate within a set time that will expire on a given date, when any money paid for the option will be forfeited.

Option ARM loan: An adjustable-rate mortgage that gives the borrower several alternative ways to make monthly payments.

Option fee: A straightforward fee the buyer pays under a lease-to-own purchase, typically anywhere from 1 to 5 percent of the price. If the option is put to use, this fee goes toward the purchase price; if not, the option is lost.

Option listing: Listing a property for sale and allowing the listing broker the choice to buy it.

Option to renew: A provision in rental contracts stating, under certain terms, the tenant can lengthen the lease.

Oral contract: A verbal agreement that cannot be enforced in real estate matters.

Ordinance: Civic regulation of land uses.

Orientation: How a building is situated in relation to prevailing winds and sun angles. The right orientation can give the building a heating or cooling advantage.

Original principal balance: The total principal owed before any payments are made on a mortgage.

Origination fee: The price a borrower pays a lender to prepare a loan.

Out parcel: A piece of land near another property that once included it. Also, a single retail property in a shopping center.

Outside of closing (paid outside closing, POC on settlements): Directly paying closing fees without following normal procedures.

Outstanding balance: Unpaid debt that is a borrower's duty to address.

Over-improvement: Using the land too intensively. This includes spending money excessively to improve the property.

Overage: Additional money beyond rent paid for leasing retail property, determined by sales success.

Overhang: Roof edge sticking out past an outer wall.

Owner financing: Occurs when a seller lends the buyer money needed to purchase his or her property.

Owner occupant: One who owns and inhabits property.

Owner's policy: In title insurance, this is the part of the policy that protects the borrower in the event something were to go wrong with the title, such as a lien missed in the title search. This policy is designed to protect the borrower against losses of this type.

Owner's title insurance: A title insurance policy for the buyer that insures the property's full purchase price. The insurance premium is paid at settlement, and coverage goes on forever.

Ownership in severalty: Possession of property by one person, considered "severed" from additional title-holders.

P

Package mortgage: Includes real estate and personal property as collateral for securing a note. Often used for collateral in creative financing for individuals.

Pad: A spot for one mobile home among others. Also, a site or foundation suitable to be improved — built upon or used — in a certain way.

Paper: A deed contract, mortgage, or note someone retrieves from the buyer after selling property.

Par rate: A reference point for mortgage lenders in which the interest rate is at zero points; there are no positive or negative adjustments to fee.

Parapet: Part of a house's wall reaching higher than the roof.

Parcel: A lot, part of a tract.

Parking ratio: A figure comparing the leasable square feet in a building to the number of parking spots.

Partial payment: An insufficient portion of a mortgage loan's monthly payment. Lenders typically do not accept partial payments, but the mortgagor may make his or her case to the loan servicing collection department in a time of need or hardship.

Partial prepayment: Paying off a loan earlier by making larger payments than scheduled or required.

Partial sale: Selling a portion of a property.

Participating broker: Finds a buyer for property listed with a different brokerage firm. Participating brokers can split payment with listing brokers.

Participation loan: A mortgage that multiple lenders share. The lender who originates the loan is the "lead" lender.

Parties: Central or primary entities in legal processes or transactions. Parties buy and sell real estate.

Partition: Court procedure to divide real estate between cotenants when they don't agree to end shared ownership.

Partnership: Two or more people who voluntarily carry on a business to make profit.

Passive income: Income gained without any effort from the person receiving the income.

Passive investor: An investor who wants to earn income through investing in funds but who does not want to take an active role in the operations.

Paydown magic: Believing there is an extraordinary or unique way to quickly pay down a home mortgage's balance if the "secret" is known.

Payee: The person to whom a note is paid.

Payer: A person, also known as a maker, who signs a note and agrees to pay it.

Payment adjustment interval: On an ARM, this is the period between changes in payments. The payment adjustment interval may or may not be the same as the interest rate adjustment period. Negative amortization could be generated on loans in which the payment is adjusted more infrequently than the rate.

Payment bond: Assures a building owner construction costs will be covered, and no one will file a mechanic's lien.

Payment cap: The maximum amount of money the monthly payment on a mortgage may increase in a period of time. Periodic caps on adjustable rate mortgages limit the amount of money the monthly payment can increase from one adjustment period to the next. Most loans also have a lifetime cap, which limits the total amount the monthly payment can increase over the term of the loan.

Payment change date: The set day when a new monthly payment is implemented for an adjustable-rate mortgage or graduated-payment mortgage. The change date for these payments usually happen the month immediately following the interest rate adjustment date.

Payment power: A Fannie Mae program that permits a borrower to miss a maximum of two mortgage payments during a 12-month period and up to a maximum of ten skipped payments during the loan's life.

Payment rate: The interest rate used to figure out the payments that must be made on the mortgage. The payment rate is typically, but not necessarily, the interest rate.

Payment shock: A considerable increase in an ARM payment that could take the borrower by surprise because of its added size. Payment shock could also refer to the sizable difference in the rent paid by someone buying a home for the first time and the monthly expense on the home being bought.

Payoff month: The month in which the balance of the loan is paid down to equal zero.

Payoff statement: A document reporting how much money a debtor must repay, in total. This statement, which the lender signs, protects the interests of both parties.

Penthouse: A luxurious dwelling on a high-rise building's uppermost floor.

Per diem interest: Due or added to each day.

Percentage lease: Used for business properties, this rental contract calls for tenants to pay a percentage of their profits to the owner when sales exceed a specific amount.

Percentage rent: Rent payments that grow or shrink depending on how successfully a commercial property makes money.

Percolation test: A way to determine if someone can use a septic system to remove waste. It tests how well soil soaks up and draws off water.

Perfecting title: Clearing a real property title of claims or clouds.

Performance bond: Posted by a contractor. Its proceeds go toward fulfilling the contract, and it ensures the contractor will fulfill all contract duties or pay the owner for losses if not.

Periodic payment cap: A set restriction on how much payments can increase or decrease over a single adjustment period. These caps are for adjustable-rate mortgages that have minimum payments and interest rates that fluctuate independently of each other.

Periodic rate cap: A set restriction on how much an interest rate for an adjustable-rate mortgage can increase or decrease during a single adjustment period for an ARM, regardless of what the index is.

Periodic refinancing: An unwise endeavor that involves occasional refinances to borrow equity for use as cash advances.

Periodic tenancy: Rental of a building one month or year at a time. Does not necessarily give the tenant any right to extend the rental period.

Permanent buydown: Decreasing the interest rate for the entire life of the loan by paying points.

Permanent financing: A lasting loan not meant to fund construction or other short-term needs.

Permissive waste (negative waste, passive waste): Occurs when tenants do not maintain their property and fix problems as realistically expected.

Perquisites (perks): A profit of some kind in addition to a normal salary, such as the use of a company car, gym membership, or entertainment allowance.

Personal property (chattel): Possessions people can carry with them — not real property.

Personal representative (executor, administrator): Someone appointed to carry out the will of a person who dies. This representative is chosen by the will itself or by the probate court.

Phase I audit: The first check for negative environmental effects on a property. Having this audit allows buyers to avoid responsibility for fixing problems they find after purchasing the real estate.

Physical life: Predicted time period that buildings or other structures on real estate will last or remain livable.

PI: In regards to a loan, this means "principal and interest."

Pier: A column holding up some edifice.

Piggyback loan: A multilender mortgage with one lender in charge. Also, a pledged long-term loan combined with a construction loan.

Pipeline risk: The risk a lender takes that, between when a borrower is presented with a lock commitment and the time when that loan is closed, interest rates could increase, and the lender would incur a loss when selling the loan.

Pipestem lot (flag lot): A slender lot forming a corridor for nearby residents to reach a road, used in places where lots fronting roads are not always available. The pipestem lot fronts the road on its short side.

Pitch: Angle, such as a roof slope. Pitch is also a black, viscous material used to patch roofs or pavement.

PITI (Principal, interest, taxes, insurance): The parts of each payment on mortgage insurance or impounded loans.

PITI reserves: The on-hand cash amount a borrower must have once a down payment is made and all closing costs are paid when buying a home. The PITI reserves have to be the same amount as what the borrower would pay for PITI in a predetermined amount of months.

Planned unit development (PUD): Has common areas and living units owned by an association, unlike a condominium, in which people own their individual units and the association owns common spaces.

Planning commission (zoning commission, zoning board, or planning board): Citizens local governments authorize to collectively create zoning laws and hold hearings.

Plans and specifications: Illustrations specifying all details of a development project, including its electrical and mechanical features, as well as orders for design and use of certain materials.

Plat: An illustration mapping borders of roads, easements, and pieces of property.

Plat book: This public record shows how tracts of land are broken down and provides the size and shape of each parcel.

Plat map: Shows property lines in a given area, such as a subdivision.

Plaza: A central public gathering space or courtyard amid a shopping center or other area.

Plot plan: A map of how a parcel is used or will be used. It details where it is, how large it is, how it is shaped, and what parking spaces and landscaping it has.

Pocket listing: Kept private by the listing broker for a time before entering the Multiple Listing Service. Delaying its entry gives that broker time to find a buyer before other brokers do.

Point: A percentage of interest on a mortgage. For example, one percent is one point. This is considered the fee the bank charges for a loan. *See also "discount points."*

Portable mortgage: Allows a borrower to transfer a mortgage from one property to another while keeping the same rate. However, the borrower must pay a premium on other loans of commensurate value, as well as appraisal fees and title insurance at the time of transfer.

Portfolio lender: Rather than selling loans, a portfolio lender keeps the loans it generates in a portfolio.

Portfolio loan: A mortgage reinstated for servicing by a bank or lender, rather than being sold to investors on the secondary market.

Positive spread investing (PSI): A common way for a public company to manage its risk while simultaneously earning a rate of return that exceeds its capital costs. For a REIT, PSI involves raising equity and debt funds at a significantly lower cost than the initial returns that can be obtained on real estate transactions. The contribution of funds to generate the PSI normally comes from three areas: investment yield, capital costs, and rate of activity.

Posted prices: The prices of mortgages distributed to mortgage brokers and loan officers by lenders, in contrast to the final prices that borrowers pay.

Potable water: Safe to drink.

Power of attorney: Written permission for someone to act as another's agent under specific terms. The agent is called an attorney-in-fact.

Power-of-sale clause: A clause in trust deeds and some mortgages. If the debtor defaults, it gives the trustee or mortgagee the right to sell the property that is security for the loan at a public sale with no court procedure.

Preapproval: A buyer with good credit can get preapproved before shopping for a home. The lender checks the borrower's credit and income to determine how much they can take in a loan. This gives the borrower a price range for home shopping but is not a guarantee for a loan.

Preapproval letter: Tells a buyer how much money a lender will loan.

Predatory lending: Using multiple shady lending methods to dupe and benefit from unsuspecting borrowers.

Preliminary title insurance report: Given by a title insurer before the insurance itself to show the company is willing to insure a title.

Premium: Extra worth beyond the face value of a bond or mortgage or extra money paid beyond market price for something excellent or desirable. Premiums are also prices of insurance coverage.

Prepaid expenses: Money handed over early for scheduled payments, such as insurance and taxes.

Prepaid interest: Interest collected at the time of closing for the balance of the month. This is a partial month's interest payment for the remainder of the current month when closing takes place.

Prepaid items: These are other costs paid at closing in addition to interest. These items can include payments for taxes and insurance that may be required by the lender.

Prepayment: Money repaid to a lender before it is required to shrink a debt.

Prepayment clause: A provision in a deed of trust or note that allows the borrower to pay off the principal before it is due, either all or in part, with or without a prepayment penalty.

Prepayment penalty: A fee borrowers must pay lenders for repaying the entire debt prematurely. Lenders charge this penalty because a buyer who pays off a loan early pays less interest and other fees.

Prequalification: A more detailed process in which the borrower provides enough financial information to secure a commitment from the lender. This process determines how much money a buyer can borrow for a mortgage. Buyers should get at least two or three lenders for prequalification.

Prequalified loan: A lender's opinion that a borrower is eligible for a given loan. Lenders interview possible borrowers and examine their credit histories to decide prequalification, but lenders must formally evaluate people's finances before loaning them money.

Presale: When people to buy homes or other structures that are planned but not yet built.

Preservation district: Zoned to conserve wildernesses and beaches, as well as managed forests, grazing sites, and historic or picturesque spots.

Prevailing rate: The average amount of interest borrowers are paying on mortgages.

Price: An expression of value in money; how much cash something is worth, not value itself.

Price-gouging: Charging exorbitant fees or interest rates in relation to the fees or rates borrowers might have found if they had spent time shopping the market.

Price-to-earnings ratio (P/E ratio): The measurement between a company's earning per share and its stock price. It is calculated by dividing the stock price by the earnings per share of the company, on either a trailing 12-month basis or a forward-looking basis.

Pricing notch point (PNP): Any growth added to a loan amount will cause the interest rate, mortgage insurance premium, or points to also increase.

Primary residence: The house the borrower lives in most of the time, as opposed to a secondary or vacation home, or certain investment properties rented out to others.

Prime rate: Cheapest interest to pay. It comes with short-term loans to banks' favored clients.

Principal: The loan amount before interest or fees are applied.

Principal balance: The remaining unsettled balance of a mortgage's principal, not including interest or other charges.

Principal broker: Someone licensed and in charge of everything a brokerage firm does.

Principal limit: A home's current value under the reverse mortgage program of the FHA, given the elderly owner's right to stay there until he or she voluntarily moves out or passes away.

Principal residence: Where a person mainly resides.

Principle of conformity: States properties are worth more if they resemble others nearby in their dimensions, appearance, functionality, and age.

Priority: Sequence of importance. High priority liens are those made first and addressed first. Tax liens beat all others in priority.

Private equity offering: Small stakes in a business sold directly to select individuals or firms but not to the general public.

Private mortgage insurance (PMI): Insurance from private companies that guards lenders against losing money if a borrower fails to repay a loan. When a borrower takes a loan for more than 80 percent of a home's price, the lender must have this insurance.

Pro forma statement: Describes financial outcomes predicted but not necessarily realized.

Pro rata: Amount of operating and upkeep costs each tenant pays based on the proportions of property they rent.

Probate: Court decision of who is heir of an estate and what assets are included.

Processing: Assembling and managing a mortgage transaction's records and information, including the appraisal, credit report, and employment and asset confirmation. The underwriting department later gets the processing file for the loan decisions.

Processing fee: Money borrowers pay lenders for collecting needed information to set up their loans.

Profit and loss statement: Describes the money a business earns and spends along with ensuing losses or profits over a certain amount of time.

Progress payments: Funds loaned to builders in installments as a construction project progresses.

Promissory note: A pledge on paper to pay off a debt by a certain date.

Property flipping: Several consecutive, fraudulent home sales, each at increasingly higher prices as part of a plot to cheat the FHA.

Property manager: A person paid to oversee another's property. This manager handles upkeep and accounting and takes rent payments.

Property reports: Government documents that describe properties for prospective buyers. Developers and subdividers compile these mandatory papers.

Property tax: Fee based on the market value of the property that is collected by the county where the property is located.

Proration: Costs assigned proportionally to the seller and the buyer when a transaction closes. These expenses are prepaid or paid at the end of a term.

Prospect: Someone expected to purchase.

Prospectus: The main disclosure document in a public offering. This is used to sell the offering to investors by giving them a detailed look at the operations of the business.

Public auction: A meeting in which the public gathers to buy property seized from a borrower to pay off a defaulted mortgage.

Public land: Federally owned. Someone can buy it if the government no longer needs it.

PUD: A type of zoning classification that includes mixed uses or various types of housing for planned unit developments.

Punch list: A list of problems to fix or features to complete for a nearly finished construction project.

Purchase agreement: Contract giving the conditions and terms of a property sale, signed by both parties.

Purchase-money mortgage: A mortgage between seller and buyer; the seller provides a purchase-money mortgage to the buyer in seller financing.

Purchase-money transaction: Paying money or its equivalent to take possession of a piece of real estate.

Purchaser's policy (owner's policy): Insurance the seller provides the buyer as required by their contract. This policy guards against problems with the title.

Q

Quadraplex: A building with four private home units.

Qualification: A borrower's eligibility for a loan based on his or her credit history and ability to repay.

Qualified acceptance: Occurs when someone takes an offer under specific conditions, adjusting or changing its terms.

Qualification rate: During the process of qualifying a borrower, this is the interest rate used to determine the beginning mortgage payment. The rate used in this situation could be a mortgage's initial rate, or it might not. For example, a borrower might be qualified at the fully indexed rate on an ARM instead of at the initial rate.

Qualifying ratio: A comparison between a borrower's income and the debt payments he or she would handle after getting a loan of a certain size. It helps lenders decide how much money to loan.

Qualification requirements: Guidelines and criterion set forth by lenders as prerequisites for giving out loans, such as the maximum ratio of a borrower's housing and total expenses in relation to income, the largest possible loan amount, and the maximum loan-to-value ratio.

Quarter section: 160 acres.

Quitclaim deed: A document that erases someone's ownership of real property and transfers it to another without any obligations and without guaranteeing the person giving it up had certain ownership.

R

R-value: A measurement of how well something provides insulation, which means blocks or conducts heat.

Radon: A natural gas implicated in lung cancer.

Range of value: The spectrum of prices a piece of real estate might be worth on the market.

Rate caps: Restrictions on how much of a rate adjustment can be applied to an ARM, frequently expressed in the following fashion: a/b/c. "A" is the largest rate change at the initial rate adjustment, "b" is the largest change for all following adjustments, and "c" represents the largest allowable increase over the first rate throughout the contract's lifetime.

Rate lock: A guarantee a lender makes not to change a borrower's interest rate for a certain time.

Rate protection: Protects a borrower from rising rates between the time of applying for a loan and closing the loan. This can be a "locked" rate, which remains the same until closing, or a "float-down" rate, which allows for declining rates if the market declines. The protection only lasts for a certain time.

Rate sheets: Lists or spreadsheets containing points and interest rates lenders deliver to mortgage brokers or loan officer employees every day.

Rate/point breakeven: The time in which a borrower must keep possession of a mortgage for it to pay well enough to pay points and lower the rate.

Rate/point options: All possible points and interest rate combinations a certain loan program offers. Interest rates and points on an ARM could differ when taking the margin and the interest rate ceiling into account.

Raw land: Undeveloped, untouched property.

Ready, willing, and able buyer: Someone who can and will accept the sales terms a property owner gives and does what is needed to close the deal.

Real estate agent: Someone with a license to coordinate sales of real property.

Real estate broker: An agent who has met educational requirements to qualify for his or her own real estate business and hire other independent agents. They will earn a commission of what the agent generates in sales volume.

Real estate contract: A contract for the purchase, sale, exchange, or conveyance of real estate between parties.

Real estate fundamentals: Things that determine property's value.

Real estate investment trust (REIT): A group of people who share ownership in a trust that invests in real estate. They receive profits from the trust and get tax breaks on income from the property.

Real Estate Investment Trust Act of 1960: The federal law that started REITs. The original goal, which carries through today in many ways, was to let small investors have the ability to pool their real estate investments so they could obtain the same benefits they might get if they directly owned the property. The REIT allows those investors to diversify their risks. REITs have to follow certain tax and dividend guidelines; otherwise the company is forced to suspend or outright relinquish its REIT status.

Real estate license law: Governs who can broker real estate in a given state to guard buyers and sellers against scams and ineptitude.

Real estate owned (REO): Real property a lender or savings institution receives because of a foreclosure.

Real estate: The physical land and anything around that is permanently attached to it, such as homes or other buildings. Sometimes called real property.

Real estate recovery fund: Created in certain states to pay parties claiming losses caused by someone holding a real estate license. Licensees contribute money to it.

Real Estate Settlement Procedures Act (RESPA): This federal law states lenders must give borrowers a reasonable approximation of what costs they will incur before they get a loan. It forbids lenders from giving or getting kickbacks and certain fees for referrals to agents specializing in real estate settlements.

Real property: Real estate and the associated rights, benefits, owned land, and improvements upon it.

Realtist: Someone part of the National Association of Real Estate Brokers (NAREB).

Realtor®: Trademarked name for an active member of the National Association of Realtors®.

Reasonable time: Amount of time that can realistically be expected for something to occur, such as parties fulfilling duties for a contract. Not including reasonable times in contracts can leave them vulnerable to legal challenges.

Recapture clause: A contract term allowing a party to take back rights or interests previously granted to others.

Recapture rate: To an appraiser, this means the rate at which someone recovers invested money.

Recast payment: Adjusting the mortgage payment on an ARM or on a variable rate mortgage to make certain the mortgage will be paid in full by the time of its maturity.

Receivables financing: A loan borrowed against a company's accounts receivable, usually a short-term, high-interest loan.

Reciprocal easements: Restrict how subdivision or development land is used in all the owners' best interests. Also, they are easements pertaining to everyone involved.

Reclamation: Altering land so it can support construction, natural resource use, or other operations, such as priming wetlands for agriculture by draining off water.

Reconveyance: Occurs when a borrower gets a title back from the lender or the lender's trustee after paying off the mortgage.

Record owner: Someone who owns a real estate title, noted in a public record.

Record title: Publicly recorded title.

Recorder: A public official who keeps track of transactions that affect real estate in a certain area. Also known as a county clerk or a registrar of deeds.

Recording: An action necessary to render a deed effective as a public notice; the entering of a debt instrument such as a mortgage into the public records. A mortgage or deed of trust is entered into the public records as proof of the debt on the property.

Recording fee: Price one pays a real estate agent for making a property sale part of public records.

Recreational lease: A lease allowing the tenant to use property for recreation. Used, for example, in large subdivision pools or sports facilities.

Rectangular (government) survey system: Surveying that uses markers called base lines and principal meridians as references to describe land. The U.S. government created this method in 1785.

Redlining: A lender discriminating illegally against borrowers in specific areas and giving them no loans even if they are eligible.

Reentry: A landlord's legal prerogative to repossess property when a tenant's lease ends.

Referral agency: Finds possible sellers and buyers and refers them to real estate agencies, which handle other tasks surrounding a sale. A referral agency comprises a group of licensed salespeople who earn money for each referral.

Referral fees: The payments service providers make to third parties in return for recommending their services or sending customers to them. A title company, for example, gives up something valuable to a lender for sending someone in need of title insurance into its service.

Referral power: Possessing the capability to recommend specific vendors to clients. Referral power largely depends on the clients' naïveté as well as on the influence of the person giving the referral.

Referral site: A website dealing with mortgages. It suggests participating lenders, sometimes hundreds of them, to prospective borrowers to familiarize themselves with their options. Referral sites are attractive to customers because of the information and general pricing offered by the lenders.

Refinance: When a new loan replaces an old one. Refinancing also means using money gained from a loan to repay another loan.

Refinance transaction: Paying the remaining balance for one loan with the money from a different loan, using the same property as security.

Registered land: Property documented within the Torrens system.

Registrar: An official record keeper who works with documents such as mortgages and deeds.

Regulation: A rule applying to procedures or management activities, which can function as a law.

Regulation D: An SEC regulation allowing certain private offerings that meet certain conditions exemption from federal registration.

Regulation Z: Obliges lenders to share all the terms and costs of a mortgage with borrowers to clarify the agreement they are undertaking. This federal legislation applies the contents of the Truth and Lending Act.

Rehab (rehabilitation, rehabilitate): A major restoration to help a structure last. To rehabilitate is to improve the condition of a building.

Rehabilitation mortgage: Pays for fixing up a building.

Reinstate: Restore something's previous status. A property owner is reinstated by getting the property back after selling it.

Reissue rate: A lowered fee from a title insurer for insurance on a property recently covered by another policy.

REIT Modernization Act of 1999: One of several important changes to the original REIT legislation. It allows a REIT to own up to 10 percent of a taxable REIT subsidiary able to offer services to REIT residents and others, a change that allows a REIT to save on expenses and operate more efficiently. The act also altered the minimum distribution requirement from 95 percent of a REIT's taxable income to 90 percent, a number consistent with the REIT rules on the books from 1960 to 1980.

Release (release of lien): Liberates real property from being collateral in a mortgage.

Release clause: A stipulation in a trust deed or blanket mortgage that permits the property owner to ensure the release of properties upon certain terms, generally the payment of a specific sum of money.

Relocation clause: A lease provision stating the landlord can transfer a tenant to a different part of the building.

Relocation company: Helps an employee move to a new city, performing services such as buying the person's new home and selling the old one. It contracts as needed with other companies to smooth the moving process.

Remaining balance: The as-yet unpaid principal amount.

Remaining term: The term or payments remaining before a loan is paid off.

Remediation: Clearing a property of environmental contaminants or lowering them to a tolerable amount.

Rendering: An artistic illustration of how an undeveloped structure will look when finished.

Renegotiation of lease: Occurs when tenant and owner discuss new terms different from what is in their existing contract.

Renewal option: A rental contract clause that gives a tenant the choice to make a lease last longer.

Rent control: Caps how much rent landlords can ask for. These government regulations are meant to control housing costs so people can afford to rent.

Rent escalation: Changes in rental fees reflecting upkeep costs for the property or living expenses.

Rent loss insurance: Fires or similar disasters can cause the leased property to be nonrentable, resulting in no rent from tenants, which in turn results in no income for the landlord. Rent loss insurance protects landlords against this type of rent or rental value loss.

Rent premium: An increase in the rent payment on a lease-to-own home purchase. If the purchase option is put to use, then the rent premium is credited to the purchase price; however, the rent premium is forfeit if the option is left unused.

Rent roll: Lists each tenant, his or her rent, and when his or her lease ends.

Rent schedule: Created by a landlord to give a tenant predictions of rent payments, as determined by market forces, expected expenses for the building, and the owner's future plans regarding the property.

Rent-to-own: A sales contract that enables a buyer to rent-to-own the property they wish to buy. Typically, a buyer will rent a property until it is paid in full, and then the deed transfers from the seller to the buyer.

Rental agency: Receives compensation to coordinate the dealings between potential tenants and landlords.

Rental agreement: A spoken or documented agreement that someone will inhabit and use a landlord's building under specific conditions and terms.

Rental growth rate: Expected changes over time in how high rental rates will be based on market forces.

Repairs: Fixing up features of a property but not trying to lengthen its useful life as a capital improvement would.

Repayment plan: An agreement made between parties to pay back overdue installments.

Replacement cost: Expectation of how much money it will take to build a new structure equal to a current one.

Replacement reserve fund: Money saved by a planned unit development, condominium, or cooperative project to replace shared parts of a building.

Representation and warranties: Indemnifications and covenants written into the purchase and sell agreement that provide important factual information necessary to protect a buyer from incidents in the future.

Reproduction cost: The current expense of building a precise double of an existing structure.

Request for proposal (RFP): Document from potential clients formally asking investment managers to describe their business records, investing tactics, fees charged, current chances for investing, and other information.

Required cash: A homebuyer needs this amount of total cash to close the transaction. Includes down payment, points and fixed charges paid to the lender, mortgage premium to be paid up front, and other settlement charges.

Rescission: One party voiding a contract, leaving both parties situated as they were before making the agreement.

Reserve account: Paid into by a borrower for the lender's protection.

Reserve fund: Holds money in escrow for a building's expected maintenance costs.

Resident manager: Someone living in an apartment building while managing it.

Resort property: Has the natural beauty or built structures for vacation and enjoyment. Examples include golf courses and resorts associated with beaches and theme parks.

Restriction: Legal constraints on how people can use a piece of land.

Restrictive covenant: A limitation on how an owner can use property, included in the deed by the party granting it.

Resubdivision: Further breaking down a subdivision to form more lots.

Retail lender: A lender who makes mortgage loans available to the public; different from a wholesale lender, who functions through connections with informants and mortgage brokers.

Retainage: Payment for a contractor's work, delayed until a certain time, such as when construction finishes.

Retaining wall: An upright barrier against moving soil or water.

Revenue stamp: Placed on a deed to show parties have paid state taxes for transferring a title.

Reverse mortgage: Allows people with valuable property to get payments from lenders drawn from the equity of their real estate.

Review appraiser: Someone from the government, a bank, or another authority who examines the contents of appraisal reports.

Revolving debt: Situation in which the debtor pays back a loan and borrows against that loan while continuing to repay it.

Rider: Something added to a contract, such as an amendment.

Right of first refusal: Given in a lease, it states the inhabitant gets the first chance to buy the rented property. It can also allow the tenant to rent more property if he or she matches reasonable terms someone else has offered the landlord for that space.

Right of ingress or egress: The ability to go into and leave from a specified establishment.

Right of survivorship: In the case of joint tenancy, right of survivorship is the ability for a survivor to obtain the interest of the deceased joint tenant.

Right of way: Permission for another to build roads on an owner's land or pass through without owning the land.

Right to rescission: Allows borrowers to back out three days or fewer after signing for a loan. This is a provision of the Truth in Lending Act. If the borrower is taking cash out at closing on a refinance loan or consolidating debts, no monies are released until after the right of recission period has passed.

Right to use: Prerogative to inhabit or use real estate, given by law.

Riparian rights: The owners who have land adjacent to water have the rights to that water source. These owners have rights to "reasonable use" of the water, which are non-transferable.

Road show: A tour of major cities in the United States by the management team and underwriters of an IPO prior to the offering date, designed to garner investment interest in the business.

ROI/ROE: To create shareholder value, "return on investment" and "return on equity" must be greater than the capital cost.

Rollover risk: Chance that renters will leave once their current lease ends.

Roof inspection clause: Included in certain sales contracts, it requires the seller to disclose what kind of roofing a home has, and any possible defects. The seller must handle repairs.

Rooming house: A home where guests pay to occupy bedrooms. Rooming houses can also allow guests use of the kitchens.

Row house: Homes attached to others on either side, meant to support one family each.

Rules and regulations: Orders describing what real estate licensees can or cannot do. They can carry the weight of law.

Runs with the land: A rule or privilege that runs with the land stays connected to the property no matter who owns it.

Rural: Not part of the heavily populated areas in and around cities.

S

S Corporation: An independent corporation owned by 35 or fewer individuals. Any profits made by the company go to the individuals without corporate-level taxes imposed.

Sale-leaseback: Involves an owner selling property then renting it from the new owner via a long-term lease.

Sales comparison approach (market data approach): Gauging a property's worth by studying the values of similar properties sold recently.

Sales contract: A document the seller and buyer sign to agree on the details of a property purchase.

Salesperson: Someone working for or with a licensed broker on real estate business.

Satellite tenant: Other renters in a mall or similar complex besides the anchor tenant — an important business using much space.

Scarcity: Low availability of something desired. Scarcity of real estate can drive up prices if many buyers are looking.

Scenario analysis: To decide in what ways an ARM payment and the interest rate will adjust or change as a result of market interest rate changes in the future, known as "scenarios."

Scheduled mortgage payment: Amount the borrower is required to pay each period, according to the mortgage contract. Includes interest, principal, and insurance. This can be fully amortizing payment throughout, interest payment only for a set number of years at the beginning of the loan, or a minimum payment based on the program.

Schematics: Sketches of project plans without final touches.

Seasoned loan: Partially paid off.

SEC: The Securities and Exchange Commission, a federal commission regulating the sale and trade of securities in the United States.

Second home: A home that is not the primary residence but is used as a vacation home. This home cannot be rented out or it is considered an investment property.

Second mortgage: Another home loan after the first one. It takes second priority for repayment.

Secondary financing: Another mortgage beyond the first one taken out to help purchase a house. Government lenders allow junior mortgages within limits.

Secondary market: The financial market in which existing mortgages are packaged and sold as mortgage backed securities. The secondary mortgage market is a major source of funding for mortgage lending.

Section 8 housing: Private rental spaces subsidized by the Department of Housing and Urban Development, so tenants only pay part of the rent.

Secure option ARM: A type of option ARM in which, instead of holding for a period of one month, the initial rate stays the same for five years.

Secured loan: A loan obtained by or supported with collateral.

Securitization: The stages of funding a pool of unrelated yet similar financial assets by issuing investor's stock for claims against the cash flow and other economic perks created by the pooled assets.

Security: Any piece of property promised as collateral when getting a loan.

Security deposit: Money tenants give a landlord when the lease begins and get back when it ends unless they damage the property or fail to pay rent.

Seed capital: The money a small business needs to start work on a prototype (alpha test) of their product in order to prove it works.

Self-employed borrower: A borrower required to keep track of all income by using tax returns instead of information the employer provides.

Seller: In a real estate agreement, the person selling his or her house.

Seller carryback: A situation in which the party selling the house lends the buyer money to purchase it.

Seller contribution: Instead of opting to reduce the price, seller contribution involves the home seller financially helping with the borrower's settlement costs or down payment.

Seller financing: The process by which the seller has agreed to finance all or some of the property for the buyer using a first or second mortgage and using a purchase-money mortgage, in most cases. *See also "seller carryback."*

Seller's expenses: The costs paid by the seller at closing in a real estate transaction. These fees include document stamps, real estate commissions, attorney's fees, surveys, cost of abstract, and escrow fees.

Seller's market: Occurs when demand for real estate rises or supply drops, allowing sellers to charge more.

Selling broker: Real estate licensee who locates a buyer.

Semidetached dwelling: A home attached to another structure by a single, "party" wall.

Senior debt: The most secure bank debt and the first in line with primary collateral. Often a short-term revolving loan paid down completely within a year.

Servicer: Collects loan payments from borrowers and handles their escrow accounts, acting for a trustee.

Servicing: To provide loans between when the loan was distributed and when it is completely paid off. Servicing also includes acquiring payments from the borrower every month, keeping and managing all documentation of loan progress, and tracking down delinquent accounts.

Servicing agent: The person delegated by a company to service a loan. He or she may or may not be the lender who originated the loan.

Servicing release premium: A fee paid to the seller by the person buying the mortgage for the release of the servicing on the mortgage. A servicing release premium holds no direct impact to the borrower.

Servicing transfer: The process of replacing one servicing agent with another.

Setback: Required space between the edge of a building and a landmark or property line in a given zone.

Settlement: *See "closing."*

Settlement costs: All expenses, including the down payment, paid by the borrower at the time of closing.

Settlement fees: *See "closing fees."*

Settlement statement: A statement given to borrowers at closing. This statement discloses all costs and fees associated with the purchase of the home. The total amount of interest paid over the life of the loan, closing costs, origination fees, and all other costs are spelled out in this statement.

Shared appreciation mortgage: A kind of mortgage in which the borrower obtains lower interest deferrals or interest rates by giving up a claim for price appreciation in the future.

Shell lease: Allows a tenant to rent an incomplete building and finish construction.

Sherman Anti-Trust Act: Federal legislation restricting trade relationships between states or with foreign countries. It aims to prevent monopolies or focus points of economic force that might harm the economy or consumers.

Shopping site: A website that allows borrowers to "shop around" and compare several competing lenders at once.

Short sale: When an owner sells property but the proceeds do not pay off his or her mortgage. The lender lets the remaining debt go and opts for less money to avoid a foreclosure.

Sick building syndrome: A problem of contaminated air in industrial or business buildings. People exposed may suffer irritated skin and eyes, upset stomachs, and headaches.

Sight line: A direction or plane of vision.

Silent second: A second mortgage the borrower does not disclose to the lender of the first.

Simple interest: The calculated interest on the loan's unpaid principal, without provisions for extra interest to be paid on interest.

Simple interest biweekly mortgage: A type of biweekly mortgage on which the payment is administered to the balance every other week instead of kept in an account as is done with a standard biweekly mortgage.

Single file mortgage insurance: A kind of mortgage insurance that requires the lender to pay the premium and charge it to the borrower in the interest rate.

Single-lender website: An individual lender or mortgage broker's website used to attract borrowers for the purpose of getting them to select a loan solely from him or her. The lender or broker's name is usually noticeably displayed on the page, which makes the site easily identifiable. The vast majority of mortgage websites are for single lenders.

Site analysis: A judgment of a parcel's usefulness for a certain purpose.

Site development: Preparation of a site for construction.

Site plan: Describes precisely where a parcel is and where builders will make improvements.

Site: Where a piece of real estate is. A site is also land beneath a structure or ground ready for construction.

Situs: Traits of a location driving the market value of a piece of real estate, including nearby properties and their effects on its worth.

Slab: The uncovered horizontal surface forming a floor, which rests atop support beams.

Slum clearance (urban renewal): Removing dilapidated buildings to make space for more beneficial land uses.

Small-claims court: Handles minor disagreements involving claims less than $1,000.

Soft money: Tax-deductable contributions to development projects or money used for fees supporting construction but not the act of building. For instance, soft money might pay architects or cover legal expenses.

Solar heating: Harnessing sunlight energy to heat water or rooms in a house.

Sole proprietorship: A situation in which one person owns a business with no other owners.

Space plan: A map of required room configurations for tenants. Space plans can describe the dimensions and layouts of rooms, including where doors are.

Spec (speculative) home: Built by a contractor who has yet to find a buyer but expects to locate a single family to purchase the home.

Special assessment: A selective levy or tax relating to a road, sewer, or other public improvement. It applies only to people whom the improvement helps.

Special conditions (contingencies): Must be fulfilled before the real estate contract containing them can bind parties involved.

Special damages: *See "actual damages."*

Special use permit (conditional use permit): Allows people to use land in ways a given zone normally would not permit.

Special warranty deed: A guarantee for buyers against flaws in a property that originated under the last owner but not other previous owners.

Specialty REIT: A REIT that owns or lends money to a type of property outside the realm of a normal REIT. A specialty REIT can own properties that include a movie theater, a timber company that owns large swaths of land, a golf course or a racetrack.

Specifications: Specific details on the construction materials, techniques, dimensions, and other elements workers must use in a project, accompanying blueprints and plans.

Spite fence: Built to irritate a neighbor. Spite fences may be abnormally high, so certain states legally limit fence heights.

Split funding: When an investor invests in two increments, usually through a down payment and a payment at another predetermined date.

Split level: A house with floors staggered so rooms in one part sit about halfway between stories in an adjacent part.

Splitting fees: Dividing money earned, which real estate brokers can do only with one another or with sellers and buyers.

Spot loan: Made to condominiums or other properties a lender has not funded before. For condominiums, securing such a loan for individual units can be difficult, and lenders might require extra payments for services like legal costs.

Spot zoning: Designating one parcel of land for different uses than other zoned property around it, an act courts might prohibit.

Square-foot method: Approximating the cost of improvements by counting the proposed square feet and multiplying by the price for one square foot of the type of construction planned.

Staging: A scaffold that supports construction materials and workers that is removed when no longer needed. Staging is also an informal term for getting homes ready to impress potential buyers.

Staking: Using pins, stakes, or paint marks to show property boundaries but not encroachments.

Standard deviation: A key measurement of risk and volatility in any portfolio. A portfolio with a low standard deviation helps bring down the overall risk but also provides lower returns.

Standard metropolitan statistical area: A county containing one or more major cities housing at least 50,000 people.

Standards of Practice: The ethical code licensed members of the National Association of Realtors® follow.

Starts: *See "housing starts."*

State-certified appraiser: Someone authorized by state government to appraise property.

Stated assets: A document specification that states a borrower's assets, but the assets are not confirmed by a lender.

Stated income: A document specification that requires the lender to confirm the borrower's source of income, but not the total amount earned.

Statute: A law the legislature enacts.

Statute of frauds: State law saying that certain contracts, deeds, and other agreements affecting title cannot be legally enforced unless they are written out and signed.

Statute of limitations: The law specifying how much time can pass before it becomes too late to bring an issue to court.

Stigmatized property: A property in which something bad occurred, which gives it a negative reputation. Certain states limit disclosure of these events, which include illness, violence, and other tragedies.

Stipulations: The terms within a written contract.

Straight lease (flat lease): Tells a tenant how much rent is due each period during the entire lease. The rent will not change.

Straight-lining: A calculation derived from the average of a tenant's rent payments over the entire lifetime of the lease. This measurement is a Generally Accepted Accounting Principles requirement for REITs.

Strategies: A system of actions, or a game plan, for success.

Straw man: One who buys property and sells it to someone else whose identity is kept secret.

Streamlined refinancing: A faster and cheaper method of refinancing that excludes several common risk control measures.

Strip center (strip mall): A line of stores too small to house an anchor tenant such as a major department store.

Structural alterations: Modification of the parts supporting a building.

Structural defects: Harm to the parts of a house bearing its weight. Structural defects make property less habitable, and they arise from earthquakes, sinkholes, and other forces shifting the ground.

Structural density: Comparison between how much floor space a building has and the lot's area. A typical industrial building has a structural density of 1 to 3, which means its land area is three times its floor space.

Studio: A living space built for efficiency that has a kitchenette, bathroom, and one main area.

Subagency: Found in Multiple Listing Service agreements, subagencies involve real estate salespeople trying to sell other agents' listed properties.

Subagent: In real estate, a salesperson authorized to work for the broker in a listing agreement. More generally, someone employed under an agent.

Subcontractor: A contractor hired for part of a construction process by the main contractor. Subcontractors often specialize in doing certain jobs.

Subdivision and development ordinances: *See "municipal ordinances."*

Subdivision: Land broken down into sections by an owner — subdivider — following a plan called a plat, which meets local land use laws. Subdivisions contain streets, blocks, and plots for buildings. Housing developments are a familiar type of subdivision.

Subject to: Taking title to property with a lien, without giving consent to personally be liable for the lien. The holder who forecloses on the lien is allowed to take the property but cannot get any money from the owner who took "subject to."

Subjective value (personal value): The price a certain person would to pay for a piece of real estate.

Sublease, subleasing, subletting: A lease contract between someone renting a space and one who rents it from the original renter. "Sub-lessee" is the term for a secondary renter.

Subordinate financing: A loan second to another in priority, taken out after the first loan.

Subordinate loan: A subsequent mortgage using the same real estate for collateral as the original loan.

Subordinated classes: Last to be paid from mortgages underlying it.

Subordination clause: Gives a mortgage priority over another mortgage recorded earlier.

Subordination: Having a lower class of security that shares the risk of losing credit with a security of a superior class. In general, subordination means placing a right, security, or something else at a lower priority or status.

Subpoena duces tecum: A court's command for someone to provide certain documents, such as records or books.

Subprime borrower: A borrower with poor credit who pays more than prime borrowers. Subprime lenders specialize in dealing with these.

Subprime lender: A lender who gives mortgages to borrowers with poor credit who do not meet the criteria for a conforming or conventional mortgage. These lenders charge higher fees and interest rates in exchange for taking on the additional risk that is associated with subprime loans.

Subprime loan: A loan with elevated fees and interest given to someone with a lower credit score.

Subprime market: The subprime lenders, investment bankers, warehouse lenders, and mortgage brokers who work with subprime borrowers.

Subprime mortgage market: Subprime lenders make loans to borrowers with poor credit. These lenders charge an interest rate significantly higher than the prime rate.

Subscribe: To sign a document at the bottom.

Subsidized housing: Living spaces partially paid for by the government, including single-family homes, apartments, and assisted-living facilities.

Substantial improvement: Increases the building's value more than 25 percent within two years. Also, substantial improvements are any made after the building has been used for at least three years.

Subsurface rights: Authority to own water, oil, gas, and other materials in the ground below a parcel of real estate.

Success coach: A motivator or speaker who focuses on building a person's self esteem.

Summary possession (eviction): When an owner takes back leased property because the tenant stays after the lease ends or breaks the rental contract.

Super jumbo mortgage: Depending on the lender, a super jumbo mortgage exceeds $650,000 or $1,000,000.

Superfund: Refers to the strict federal law requiring entities to clean up environmental hazards on property they once owned. The Superfund list includes those obligated to remove such hazards.

Surcharge: An extra fee a tenant must pay for using more electricity or other utilities than a lease allows.

Surety bond: Formed when a bonding or insurance firm promises to bear responsibility for debts, defaults, or other burdens. Surety bonds regarding real property can guarantee a contract will be fulfilled or a construction project finished on time.

Surety: Someone who knowingly gets involved in another's debt or commitment.

Surface water: Storm water in the ground not channeled into streams.

Surrender: Voiding of a rental contract by agreement of the landlord and tenant.

Survey: Method of measuring the area and borders of land. Surveys note a house's position and size, the boundaries of a lot, easements affecting property, and any structures intruding on a lot — encroachments.

Survivorship: The right for a person sharing home ownership to continue possessing the property if the second owner dies.

Sweat equity: A nickname for the labor an owner invests to improve property.

Takeout financing: Required by construction lenders, takeout financing is a pledge to finance a construction project permanently once it is complete. To receive it, the building must have a certain number of units bought or meet other requirements.

Tangible personal property: Not real estate — any possession one can touch, move, and see.

Tangible property: Visible and touchable like tangible personal property but including immovable possessions like real estate.

Target: The finish line of a goal.

Tax base: The summed worth of all the property a taxing authority manages.

Tax certificate: Given to someone to prove he paid property taxes and to show his or her right to receive the deed, with proper timing and circumstances.

Tax deed: Transfers a property to a new buyer after the owner loses it for neglecting tax payments. Properties are transferred using tax deeds if the previous owner does not pay the due taxes during a certain redemption period.

Tax deferred exchange (tax-free exchange or 1031 exchange): Trading of a property for the pledge to supply a similar one later, allowing someone taking part to avoid taxes on the first piece of real estate.

Tax lien: A claim the federal government makes against a piece of real estate to induce its owner to pay neglected taxes.

Tax map: A record kept by courthouses and tax offices that maps a parcel's size, shape, location, and other details relevant to taxation.

Tax rate: The proportion of something's value one must pay as tax.

Tax Reform Act of 1986: A federal law that allowed REITs to oversee and run most types of income-producing commercial properties, as opposed to straight-up ownership. The law is considered one of the more significant pieces of REIT legislation.

Tax sale: Selling of real property because the owner fails to pay taxes. Courts decide if tax sales occur.

Tax service fee: The closing fees some lenders charge to make sure the costs of paying taxes on the property of the borrower are covered once they come due. Tax service fees can also be

used to confirm payments have been made on the property if
the borrower is the one paying the taxes.

Teaser rate: A temporary, cheap interest rate meant to entice
people to take out mortgages.

Temporary buydown: A discount in the payment of a mortgage
in the loan's early years in order to get advance cash payment
from the home seller, buyer, or both.

Temporary lender: A type of lender who lets go of the loans
he or she originates by selling them, as opposed to a portfolio
lender who keeps the loans he or she originates.

Tenancy at sufferance: Occurs when someone holds onto a
property without permission after a lease ends.

Tenancy at will: Living on an owner's property with
permission, which can be revoked whenever the owner chooses.
The tenant is also free to leave at will.

Tenancy by the entirety: Shared property ownership by
married couples when they wed. One spouse gets full
ownership if the other dies. Not every state recognizes tenancy
by the entirety.

Tenancy in common: Involves a group of people owning
property, with each person having a separate — not shared —
interest and the ability to leave it to an heir. Each person is the
exclusive owner of one part of the property.

Tenant (lessee): Someone with rights to buildings or land through renting or ownership.

Tenant at will: Someone a landowner permits to occupy the property.

Tenant contributions: Money or service a tenant provides beyond paying rent, mandatory under the lease.

Tenant improvement (TI): Positive changes to property made by renters or people working for them.

Tenant improvement allowance: Money a landlord provides for tenants to repair and upgrade rented property.

Tenant in common: A structured deal that allows individual investors to pool their money to buy commercial properties and other large real estate holdings, leaving the management of the actual building to another entity. Also known as a 1031 exchange.

Tender: To provide something — such as money or materials — or fulfill an obligation or contract requirement.

Tenement: Items permanently affixed to buildings or land. Tenements are also long-standing apartments.

Tenure annuity: Accessible to borrowers under a Home Equity Conversion Mortgage, this option allows them to take an established monthly amount for the entire time they live in their house.

Term: The period of time used to determine the mortgage payment for each month. The term is typically, but not always, the same amount of time as the maturity.

Termite inspection: A professional check for signs of invading termites. Loans backed by the FHA necessitate these inspections, and real estate contracts might suggest them.

Termite shield: A metal barrier meant to bar termites from a house.

Testimonium: An ending clause stating parties have officially transferred property by signing the contract on the date given.

Thin market (limited market): Has low sales rates and a few people buying and selling.

Third party: Someone indirectly involved in or related to a transaction, contract, or other interaction.

Third-party origination: The method by which a lender uses a third party to fully or partially formulate, underwrite, process, finance, close, or package the mortgages he or she intends to transfer to the secondary mortgage market.

Time is of the essence: A contract expression meaning something must be done as soon as possible.

Time value of money: Means that money brings more enjoyment and use in the present than the future and has more value now.

Time-share ownership plan: Involves tenants sharing property but using it at different times of year. Usually used for vacation purposes.

Title: Ownership of real estate, or proof thereof.

Title company: A company that insures titles and resolves who owns them.

Title exam: Investigation verifying a seller's ownership of property appears in public records. It reveals any encumbrances the property bears.

Title insurance: It protects property buyers against flaws or legal problems that come with their real estate, if the policy mentions them.

Title report: An early description of a title, not including its ownership history.

Title search: Searching public records to find and reveal any potential problems that might hinder the passing of property to a new owner.

Topography: The shape and elevation across a piece of land.

Torrens System: A way of resolving conflicts over land ownership. Only certain states require brokers to work using the Torrens System.

Total expense ratio: It compares the money one owes each month to one's earnings with expenses and taxes subtracted.

Total housing expense: The sum of the housing expense plus the monthly debt service.

Total interest payments: Adding all interest payments over the entire life of the loan or the interest payments to date. Total interest payments do not include upfront payments made in cash and are not adjusted for the time value of money. They are, therefore, an insufficient way to measure the credit cost to the borrower.

Total inventory: Entire area of useable space at a property.

Total lender fees: Payment a lender requires for putting together a loan.

Total monthly housing costs: Monthly mortgage payments plus home-related insurance, real estate taxes, and any other monthly expenses of owning a home.

Townhouse: A dwelling — not a condominium — joined to others. This type of residential home shares walls with at least one other unit and typically has two or more floors per unit.

Township: A square containing 36 square miles used for government surveying.

Township lines: East-west survey lines separated by six miles. Run parallel to the edge of a piece of land.

Township tiers: Land strips between township lines, given numbers showing how far south or north they are.

Tract house: Has a similar layout and style to surrounding homes.

Tract: Land subdivided — broken down.

Trade fixture: A possession affixed to a commercial property that one can detach when the rental contract ends.

Transaction: In real estate, the actual real estate deed.

Transfer of ownership: When a property's ownership changes between two parties. All of the following circumstances are deemed to be the transfer of ownership by lenders: buying a property contingent on the mortgage, when the buyer of the property acquires the mortgage debt, and the trading of the property's title under a land sales agreement or another land trust device.

Transfer tax: Taken by state or federal officials when real estate changes hands.

Treasury index: Serves as a basis for changing interest rates on adjustable-rate mortgages.

Treble damages: Tripled from their original amount by legal processes allowed in particular states.

Trespass: Taking or coming onto land illegally.

Triple net lease ("NNN"): Necessitates the renter pay taxes, insurance, and utilities in addition to rent.

Triplex: Contains three dwellings.

Truss: A frame supporting a roof with widely spaced beams.

Trust account: The same as an escrow account in certain states. It contains all the money a broker gathers for customers and holds it back for specific uses.

Trust deed (deed of trust): Involves a borrower entrusting a title to a lender. If the borrower does not repay the loan, the lender can sell the title publicly.

Trustee: A reliable person entrusted to hold or manage a property for another's benefit.

Truth in Lending Act: U.S. government law saying lenders must provide documents honestly describing the details of a mortgage.

Turnkey project: Has someone besides the owner in charge of building or improving a structure; for example, a project the developer finishes to the last detail. Also, a purchased property already stocked with furnishings or other objects is a turnkey property.

Turnover: How quickly properties sell or how often people leave their rented homes or jobs.

Two-step mortgage: An adjustable-rate mortgage in which the interest rate changes periodically. It could have a certain interest rate for the first five to seven years of its term and a different interest rate for the rest of its term.

Two- to four-family property: A property on which a building supplies accommodations for two to four families. The building's ownership is outlined in one deed.

U

Umbrella Partnership REIT (UPREIT): This is an operating partnership in which the partners of one REIT team up with the principles of another, newer REIT. For interests of both parties in the operating partnership, the partners from the older REIT contribute the properties while the new REIT contributes the money from its public offering. After a given period of time has passed, often one year, the partners are allowed to have the same liquidity as the REIT shareholders through selling their pieces of the partnership for either cash or REIT shares. Also, when a partner in this partnership possesses the units until death, the federal estate tax allows the beneficiaries to sell the units for cash or REIT shares without paying income tax.

Under contract: When a seller is under contract, it means he or she is committed to the transaction with a certain buyer and unable to choose another.

Under-floor ducts: Passages for phone and electricity wires beneath a floor that allow businesses or offices choices of how to arrange devices using these lines.

Under-improvement: Something constructed that does not take full advantage of the property where it is.

Underage: Money gathered by a loan officer from a borrower. These fees are cheaper than the target fees stipulated by the mortgage broker or lender who provides employment for the loan officer.

Underground storage tank: Holds water, gasoline, unwanted substances, or other liquids underground.

Undersigned: One whose name appears at the end of a document he or she signed.

Underwriters: Based on the credit and value of an applicant's loan collateral, underwriters provide advice on whether or not to make a loan approval. They are employed by mortgage lenders.

Underwriting: Involves lenders determining what terms and conditions to set on loans based on the risks each borrower presents.

Underwriting fee: Covers the expenses mortgage lenders pay to validate borrowers' personal information and choose who receives a loan.

Underwriting requirements: Standards to see if a borrower qualifies for a loan, including an evaluation of creditworthiness.

Undisclosed agency: Only allowed in certain states. It involves one real estate agent representing both parties in a transaction and not revealing the double allegiance.

Undivided interest: Shared property on which no co-owner gets any part all to himself.

Unencumbered: Free from anything making property less useful or enjoyable, such as legal claims.

Unenforceable contract: Unsigned or otherwise useless for starting a lawsuit.

Unfair and deceptive practices: Intentional lies, misleading statements, and other harmful or unethical acts.

Uniform Building Code (UBC): Provides national building standards. It is known for its use in the western United States.

Uniform Commercial Code (UCC): Set of legal rules about commerce that standardizes financial transactions between states. This code governs warranties, doing business, selling property or entire businesses, loaning money, and other commercial doings. Every state except Louisiana uses a version of UCC.

Uniform Residential Appraisal Report (URAR): A form for presenting appraisal results for a certain building. Crucial for purchasing secondary mortgages.

Uniform Settlement Statement: Given to the buyer and seller in transactions involving federal loans. It shows the amounts of money both parties will pay in closing their deal.

Unmarketable title: A seriously flawed title.

Unrecorded deed: Undocumented transfer of property ownership.

Unsecured loan: Given based on a borrower's good credit, not any collateral property.

Up-zoning: Classifying property as having higher usage than it was considered to have before.

Upfront mortgage Broker (UMB): A mortgage broker who establishes a flat rate for services and provides it in writing at the beginning of the business deal. This type of broker also acts as an agent to the borrower when searching for the best deal.

Upgrades: Improvements or alterations made before a sale's closing date and paid for by the buyer.

Upside down: A nickname for the situation where a borrower accumulates more debt than his or her property is worth.

Urban renewal (slum clearance): Destroying dilapidated city buildings and constructing new ones.

Urban sprawl: Development spreading from a city. It is sparser than the urban center and it can house people who work in the city.

Usable square footage: All the area within a tenant's living unit.

Use tax: Taken from those who import or buy tangible possessions.

Useful life: The time period before a building depreciates or stops making money.

Usury: The practice of charging an illegally high rate of interest.

Utility easement: Allows water, sewage, electric, or other utility lines to pass through someone's property.

V

VA loan: Made through a lender authorized by the Department of Veterans Affairs. A VA loan provides a safe way for financing veterans who qualify.

Vacancy factor: Percentage of future gross income expected to be lost because living spaces remain empty.

Vacancy rate: What proportion of total rental spaces is vacant.

Valid contract: Can be legally enforced because it has all the necessary parts of a working contract.

Valuable consideration: Allows someone receiving a promise to make claims on the money or time of a person who does not fulfill their pledge.

Valuation: Approximate worth or price. This is the practice of appraising to determine value.

Value-added: The worth a property is expected to gain after improvement or repair.

Variable payment plan: A schedule for repaying a mortgage with varying monthly payment.

Variable rate: Interest rate not at a locked-in rate that will vary based on the prime rate. *See also "adjustable-rate mortgage."*

Variance: Like a special uses permit, variance allows someone to improve or use property in ways the current zoning rules forbid.

Vendee: A buyer.

Vendor: A seller.

Vendor's lien: A claim on land the seller holds until the buyer fully pays for the property.

Veneer: A layer of brick, wood, or other material hiding a less preferred surface.

Venture capital: Money from venture capital funds are given to growing businesses in exchange for substantial portions of equity and control.

Verification: Made when parties swear their contract or other document contains no lies. Verification requires a qualified witness.

Verification of deposit (VOD): A statement of a borrower's account history and current status, given by banks.

Verification of employment (VOE): A document confirming a loan recipient works at a given job. The employer signs this statement.

Vested: Having the right to use all or part of a reserve of money, such as a retirement fund. For instance, a person who is 100 percent vested can take out all the money placed aside for him or her in a retirement fund. However, taxes might be imposed on withdrawn funds.

Vestibule: An entryway opening onto a larger room.

Veterans Administration (VA): Designed to provide affordable loans to eligible U.S. veterans who serve on active duty for more than 120 days. Veterans can get loans without down payments from this federal agency.

Villa: A living unit having one story, a yard, and parking spots. Villas can group in twos and fours or form condominiums.

Visual rights: The right to preserve pleasing views, keeping them free of large signs or other obstructions.

Volatility: The fluctuation of a stock price, from day-to-day, or sometimes from hour to hour. Volatility is a key factor investors look at when deciding if, and how much, to invest in a REIT.

tary lien: A claim on a piece of real estate that the owner ws and recognizes.

W

Wainscoting: A surface along the bottom of an inner wall.

Waive escrows: When a lender allows the borrower to directly pay taxes and insurance. Normally, the lender adds a monthly charge to the payment deposited in an escrow account, which allows the lender to pay the borrower's taxes and insurance.

Walk-up: A tall apartment complex in which people must use the stairs for lack of an elevator.

Walkthrough: A visit to a home by the buyer before closing the deal. The buyer makes sure the property is unoccupied and free from unexpected defects.

Warehouse fee: Paid at closing, this fee is charged by a lender for keeping a borrower's mortgage before selling it to secondary buyers.

Warehouse lender: A business that loans to temporary lenders against some form of security or collateral of closed mortgage loans before selling the loans in the secondary market. This state of flux is known as being "in the warehouse," and warehouse lenders can call these loans if they lose value while in such a state.

Warrantable condos: A condominium project protected against threats to its value for lenders. Includes insurance coverage, a majority of sold units compared to rented ones, and an independent ownership group.

Warranty deed: Guarantees the person giving the deed will guard the recipient against all possible claims.

Waste line: Drains the water from sinks, showers, and other plumbing fixtures besides toilets.

Water rights: Possessed by people living on bodies of water, these rights describe how owners can and cannot use nearby water sources.

Water table: The higher levels where water rests in the ground over a certain area.

Way: A passage for vehicles or pedestrians, such as an alley or street.

Wear and tear: Weathering of property from the elements, its age, or from people using it.

Weep hole: Small drains in walls for extra water.

Weighted Average Cost of Capital (WACC): The weighted average of a REIT's debt and equity costs. This is important for investors because if a company's WACC projects a positive cash flow looking ahead, that is a good sign for a good investment. If the projections are negative, then the investment likely has weak potential.

Weighted average rental rates: Averages and compares the different rental rates of at least two buildings.

Wetland: Swamps, marshes, and other water-filled lands protected from development by environmental laws.

Wholesale lender: These lenders have funds to lend and use mortgage brokers to secure loans for them. Some large lenders have both a wholesale division that works with brokers and a retail division that offers loans to the general public. Wholesale lenders generally have lower interest rates.

Wholesale mortgage prices: The points and interest rates that wholesale lenders quote to correspondent lenders and mortgage brokers.

Wholesaling: Property sold under market value to turn it over quickly for profit.

Will: A document that transfers property to another, the testator, when the will's creator dies.

Without recourse: A phrase meaning a borrower cannot appeal to a borrower after failing to pay debts. Rather, the lender can take the property.

Work letter: Given to a tenant by a landlord. It details which improvements the landlord will take care of and which ones the tenant must handle.

Workers' compensation acts: Require employers to insure their employees against injuries at work.

Working capital: The balance between current assets and current liabilities represents the fund available to grow the business in the short term.

Working drawings: Exact illustrations and details of how a construction project will progress.

Workout assumption: Taking on a mortgage from a borrower who is no longer able to keep up with payments, as long as there is permission from the lender.

Worst-case scenario: Assuming an ARM's interest rate will increase to the fullest amount allowed on the note. For example, on a one-month ARM that has no rate adjustment caps, its rate would leap up to the highest possible rate specified in the note in the second month.

Wraparound debt: Involves a specific agreement by the lender and borrower: A borrower pays debts on a mortgage using loaned money from the mortgage lender, which is then called a wraparound lender. The loan used to pay mortgage debt "wraps around" the mortgage itself. A promissory note and mortgage document are needed to secure this type of loan.

Wraparound mortgage: A mortgage that takes in the seller's old mortgage and covers the buyer's new loan for the property being sold.

Writ of execution: Allows real estate to be sold based on a court decision.

Write-off: In accounting, an asset lost because it cannot be collected.

XYZ

X: Can replace a signature of an illiterate person, if witnessed and affirmed by a notary.

X bracing: Bracing across a panel or divider.

Year-to-year tenancy: Involves renting property one year at a time, which can be called periodic tenancy.

Yield: Money regained from an investment through interest and dividends.

Yield curve: A type of graph that portrays how the yield changes at any given point in time until a bond reaches maturity. The yield curve typically shows an upward slope, but it can also slope downward or be flat. A flat "curve" means that long-term bond yields are scarcely higher than those of short-term notes.

Yield rate: Yield that represents a percentage of the total investment. Also called "rate of return."

Yield spread: Variation in money earned by commercial mortgages as compared to standard values. Yield spread also compares wholesale mortgage rates with retail mortgage rates. Maintaining this spread allows mortgage brokers to earn money.

Zone condemnation: Clearing out areas by knocking down structures to make space for new buildings.

Zone of Transition: The central business district's surrounding neighborhoods in a city.

Zoning: Dividing cities or towns into areas meant for different kinds of buildings or uses laws and regulations dictate.

Zoning ordinance: Laws and regulations specifying how people can use or build upon land in a certain zone.

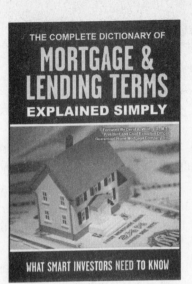

More Great Reference Dictionaries

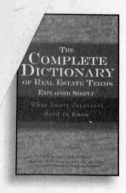

THE COMPLETE DICTIONARY OF REAL ESTATE TERMS EXPLAINED SIMPLY:
What Smart Investors Need to Know

Real estate words and real estate terms can be very confusing. Both experienced real estate investors and consumers will love this A-to-Z guide packed with more than 2,400 complicated terms easily defined. No categories are overlooked. Find all the answers you'll ever need to a universe of real estate terms on thousands of subjects, such as: abstract of title, wraparound debt, caveat emptor, escheat, metes and bounds, pipestem lot, recital, testator, devisee, and 2,400 more. This new book is designed to assist real estate agents, consumers, and investors. This new, handy guide will simplify these complicated and confusing terms for quick and easy understanding. You will not find lengthy and difficult words in the description, just short and easy to understand answers.

ISBN-13: 978-0-910627-01-6 • 288 Pgs • $21.95 • 2007 RELEASE

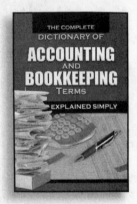

THE COMPLETE DICTIONARY OF ACCOUNTING & BOOKKEEPING TERMS
Explained Simply

This book was written for every small business owner who feels they do not have a full grasp of profits, expenses, payroll, and taxes and would like to take control. You will learn how to understand and speak the language of your accountant and bookkeeper or to take over the process yourself. Learn the different abbreviations used in the industry and what you will need to properly use this book, from the proper times to use terminology to the effective means by which to fill out your tax forms, records, and other forms. Finally, benefit from the table of detailed accounting information, from conversion charts to up-to-date tax information so that you can start understanding the complex world of your bookkeeping today and take control of your finances.

ISBN 13: 978-1-60138-325-9 • $24.95 • 288 Pgs • $24.95 • 2011 RELEASE

To order call toll-free **800-814-1132** or visit **www.atlantic-pub.com**

The Best References for Small Business

THE ENCYCLOPEDIA OF SMALL BUSINESS FORMS AND AGREEMENTS: *A Complete Kit of Ready-to-Use Business Checklists, Worksheets, Forms, Contracts, and Human Resource Documents With Companion CD-ROM*

Those who wish they had a resource for every possible small business form and agreement they have ever encountered can breathe a sigh of relief. This book is the answer, as it will provide small business owners with ready-to-use checklists, worksheets, forms, contracts, and human resource documents. Inside these pages you will find over 250 essential documents for all your hiring, firing, intellectual property, Internet, technology, legal, merger, acquisition, money, fundraising, sales, marketing, and starting a business needs. In essence, this book is a small business survival kit packed with materials you can use for every aspect of your job.

ISBN 13: 978-1-60138-248-1 • 288 Pgs • $29.95 • 2011 RELEASE

EMPLOYEE BODY LANGUAGE REVEALED: *How to Predict Behavior in the Workplace by Reading and Understanding Body Language*

Only 7 percent of communication is verbal and 38 percent is vocal (pitch, speed, volume, tone of voice). The largest chunk then, 55 percent, is visual (body language, eye contact). People form 90 percent of their opinion about you within the first 90 seconds of meeting you. Understanding body language can be a plus in the workplace. You can interpret a person's thoughts and feelings from their body language. This new book will make you an expert. Would you like to know if an employee or co-worker is lying, how to make instant friends, and persuade and influence others? This book will show you how, as well as how to transmit only the messages you want and how to use body language to your benefit in the workplace and in everyday situations.

ISBN 13: 978-1-60138-147-7 • 288 Pgs • $21.95 • 2011 Release

To order call toll-free **800-814-1132** or visit **www.atlantic-pub.com**

The Best References for Real Estate

THE COMPLETE GUIDE TO REAL ESTATE SYNDICATION: *Everything You Need to Know Explained Simply*

In this book, you'll learn what a syndicate is and the various types and needs they have. Learn the basics of syndicators, including various issues such as issuer versus dealer concerns, leverage, risks and responsibilities, choices of projects, and disadvantages of syndication. You will learn how to select a broker, negotiate financing, select a form of entity, know your tax considerations, form your entity, and document your syndicate. You will be shown how to draft provisions, manage the syndicate, market shares, ensure guarantees and securities, analyze an offering, and more.

ISBN-13: 978-1-60138-387-7 • 288 Pgs • $24.95 • 2011 RELEASE

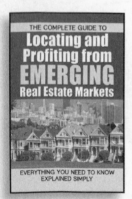

THE COMPLETE GUIDE TO LOCATING AND PROFITING FROM EMERGING REAL ESTATE MARKETS: *Everything You Need to Know Explained Simply*

With this book, anyone interested in starting their investment strategy in emerging real estate markets can start the process immediately without wasting any time or effort on false promises. You will start by learning why emerging markets are considered so lucrative and what kind of fundamental value they hold. You will learn how individuals can go about identifying these markets using the market phase method. You will learn how to start recognizing the good and bad spots in emerging markets and to get the first deal in any emerging market. You will learn the difference between single and multi-family investments and how to start paying for property managers. Every detail you could need to learn about and start capitalizing on emerging markets is included here in this guide for you.

ISBN-13: 978-1-60138-388-4 • 288 Pgs • $24.95 • 2011 RELEASE

To order call toll-free 800-814-1132 or visit www.atlantic-pub.com

The Best References for Real Estate

THE COMPLETE GUIDE TO INVESTING IN PRE-FORECLOSURE SHORT SALES:
Everything You Need to Know Explained Simply

In recent years, the number of foreclosures in the United States have increased. For that reason, many real estate investors have turned to the possibility of short sales and making money on homes that have not yet gone into foreclosure. This practice, which is ideal for helping both the banks and the homeowners on the brink of foreclosure, is a great way to take advantage of current market conditions and make greater profits. This book will work to guide any real estate veteran or beginner in the process of pre-foreclosure short sales and how to get into the market, contacting banks and owners, making offers, and taking advantage of timing and the right situations. You will learn the basics about what foreclosure is and why it is such a major occurrence and concern in today's real estate market.

ISBN-13: 978-1-60138-389-1 • 288 Pgs • $24.95 • 2011 RELEASE

SELL YOUR HOME NOW: *The Complete Guide to Overcoming Common Mistakes, Selling Faster, and Making More Money*

Put your home at the head of the market with the help of Laura Riddle's expertise. Riddle, a masters-level, award-winning real estate broker, walks today's home sellers through everything they need to know to get the best price in today's real estate market. This complete guide includes techniques for selling up to 80 percent faster, advertising to sell for 15 to 20 percent more, where to list your home online to get the most exposure, staging the home for the quickest sale, gaining an advantage over foreclosures in your neighborhood, common mistakes home sellers often make that could hinder your efforts, contracts and home Inspection reports, and more.

ISBN 13:978-1-60138-025-8 • 288 Pgs • $24.95 • 2010 RELEASE

To order call toll-free **800-814-1132** or visit **www.atlantic-pub.com**

The Best References for Investing

WALL STREET LINGO: *Thousands of Investment Terms Explained Simply*

This book does more than define terms — it explains them in a way that traditional dictionaries cannot. Where other dictionaries start at A and end at Z, *Wall Street Lingo* is organized in chapters by subject. There are over 1,000 terms investors need to know and understand. The definitions are organized by topic and fully indexed and cross-referenced. You will find an exhaustive list of commonly used acronyms and helpful resources, complete with websites. Whether you are an experienced investor or just starting out, you will appreciate the easy reading style and unique structure of this innovative investment tool.

ISBN-13: 978-1-60138-038-8 • 288 Pgs • $24.95 • 2007 RELEASE
SPANISH VERSION • ISBN-13: 978-1-60138-039-5 • 288 Pgs • $24.95 • 2008 RELEASE

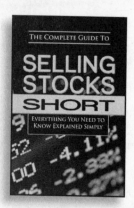

THE COMPLETE GUIDE TO SELLING STOCKS SHORT: *Everything You Need to Know Explained Simply*

With this guide both beginners and veteran investors will learn how to start selling stocks short and what the concept entails. You will learn how to read the market and what it means when they go up and down, plus how to read those fluctuations before you even start making trades. You will learn what you need to do with a rally and which stocks should be sold short and which ones should not. You will learn the fundamental aspects of how cycles work and how to time your short sales. The basics of overhead supply will be discussed along with head and shoulders taps. You will be shown the process of setting your price limits and knowing how to read and maintain those limits. Top stock brokers and home trading experts have been interviewed for this book, and their expertise has been compiled to provide you a complete look at the world of short selling.

ISBN-13: 978-1-60138-326-6 • $24.95 • 288 Pgs • $24.95 • 2011 RELEASE

To order call toll-free **800-814-1132** or visit **www.atlantic-pub.com**